Redeeming Singleness

Redeeming Singleness

*Postmodern Pastoral Care and Counseling
for Never-Married Single Women*

HyoJu Lee

WIPF & STOCK · Eugene, Oregon

REDEEMING SINGLENESS
Postmodern Pastoral Care and Counseling for Never-Married Single Women

Copyright © 2017 HyoJu Lee. All rights reserved. Except for brief quotations in critical publications or reviews, no part of this book may be reproduced in any manner without prior written permission from the publisher. Write: Permissions, Wipf and Stock Publishers, 199 W. 8th Ave., Suite 3, Eugene, OR 97401.

Wipf & Stock
An Imprint of Wipf and Stock Publishers
199 W. 8th Ave., Suite 3
Eugene, OR 97401

www.wipfandstock.com

PAPERBACK ISBN: 978-1-5326-1325-8
HARDCOVER ISBN: 978-1-5326-1327-2
EBOOK ISBN: 978-1-5326-1326-5

Manufactured in the U.S.A.   DECEMBER 13, 2016

Contents

Acknowledgments | vii

Chapter 1   Introduction | 1

    1.1. Introduction
    1.2. Discussion of the Issue
    1.3. The Audience of the Study

Chapter 2   From Modernity to Postmodernity | 11

    2.1. Introduction
    2.2. Incredulity toward Big Stories
    2.3. A Description of Postmodern
    2.4. The Confidence of Modernity
    2.5. Guarantor of Modern Confidence: The Ethos of Objectivity
    2.6. Erosion of the Ethos of Objectivity

Chapter 3   The Influence of Postmodernity on the Field of Pastoral Care and Counseling | 35

    3.1. Shifts within the Field of Pastoral Care and Counseling
    3.2. Literatures on Singleness

Chapter 4   Research Methods | 45

    4.1. Introduction
    4.2. Qualitative Research and Practical Theology
    4.3. Construction of Data
    4.4. Coding and Analysis
    4.5. Emergent Themes

4.6. Credibility
4.7. Co-Constructors of the Data
4.8. Confidentiality
4.9. Limitations and Contributions

Chapter 5   Pastoral Care and Counseling and Postmodernism | 58
5.1. Introduction
5.2. The Issue of Oppression and Marginalization in Light of Pastoral Practices
5.3. Invisible Oppression
5.4. Dominant Discourse vs. Subordinate Discourse
5.5. Social Constructionism
5.6. Social Construction of the Concept of Marriage and Family
5.7. Social Constructivist Influence on the Concept of Therapy

Chapter 6   Narratives: Powerful Instruments for Pastoral Practices | 89
6.1. Introduction
6.2. Why Metaphors?
6.3. Why the Metaphors of Narratives?
6.4. Finding the Concealed Stars
6.5. Re-Constellations

Chapter 7   A Vision for Churches | 115
7.1. Introduction
7.2. Ecclesiology and Pastoral Practices
7.3. Lived Experiences of My Research Partners
7.4. Church as an A Cappella Choir
7.5. Counter-Communities as a Source of Resistance
7.6. The Notions of Divine Hospitality and Alterity
7.7. Conclusion

Appendix A   *Email to send to my acquaintances* | *141*
Appendix B   *Email to send out to churches in the Los Angeles area* | *143*
Appendix C   *Interview Consent Form* | *145*
Appendix D   *Emergent Themes with Master Codes* | *149*

Bibliography | *151*

Acknowledgments

TWELVE YEARS CAN BE a short time. It can also be a long time. For me, it has been quite a journey toward completing my Ph.D. degree. Of course, my life before these twelve years matters. Yet, I just want to look back on the past twelve years, the second chapter of my life, while I write these acknowledgements. I always realize the shortcomings of human language when I need to say a few words to those to whom I feel profoundly indebted. The words, *thank you*, are not enough to deliver what I feel. That is why I have delayed writing this part of my dissertation. Nevertheless, I want to say a few words to express my gratitude.

During these past 12 years, I have gained far more than I could have ever expected or imagined. The theme of the second chapter of my life would be "transformation." In this foreign land, it seems as if I have given birth to myself. When I decided to come here to study abroad, I vaguely wished to finish a doctoral degree someday, but I was not quite sure how to get there. I have depended on total strangers' hospitality, strangers who embraced me and helped me to flower into my unique colors and shapes. I am deeply grateful for unknown donors whose generosity made my education possible at Drew University and Claremont School of Theology. They have shown me a model of how to live my life paying it forward.

Specifically, I am thankful for my advisor, Dr. Duane Bidwell, whose energy filled with humor has empowered me to continue to think freshly and write diligently. His encouragement enabled me to continue when I wanted to give up. I appreciate his feedback given in a timely manner. My gratitude extends as well to Dr. Samuel Lee and Dr. Rosemary Radford Ruether. Dr. Lee has been kindly encouraging me to feel a sense of family.

His feedback has sharpened my methodology in particular. Dr. Ruether has shown me how a radical theologian can age with grace and understanding. I also want to say thank you to Dr. Kathleen Greider, whose teaching has been inspiring to me.

Further, I am forever thankful for the process of Clinical Pastoral Education at Mercy Medical Center in Rockville Centre, New York. I want to say a special thank you to Sr. Normajean Lokcinski, who mentored me and has walked with me through her prayers. When it comes to prayer, I cannot help but remember my sisters and brother, Eunju, Youngju and Seokju, in South Korea. I know that Kyungho, another sister, and my father, who both passed away while I was in the United States would be very happy to see me completing my degree. I am grateful for my close friends who have been like my second family here in California: Dr. KyungSik Park, Dr. Jingu Kwon, Sunghwan Lee, Kyuwook Lee, Hyejin Kwon and Hyeli Suh. I am also thankful to Dr. Vicki Wiltse, my proofreader, who has walked with me despite bumps here and there. Although I cannot mention all my friends both in South Korea and in the States, my thanks are immeasurable. The gratitude and indebtedness in my heart will be where I start writing the third chapter of my life.

Chapter 1

Introduction

1.1. Introduction

A DEROGATORY NICKNAME FOR Jesus was, "a friend of tax collectors and sinners."[1] Jesus was not afraid to hang out with people who were relegated to the margins of society and considered second-class citizens. He dared to drink and dine with them, instead of trying to correct them in terms of religious and societal norms. Jesus invited people from the margins of society to the fellowship table as people created in God's image, showing them respect and love. I believe that if Jesus were living in today's world, his focus would still be on the margins of society. This impels me to ask, "Who is at the margins of today's church? Who is excluded from the conversations? Why?" and, "Are there ways to restore 'Jesus' radical practice of open table fellowship,[2] by inviting the marginalized to a place where they are heard and recognized as a necessary part of the bigger community?"

As I have dwelt on these questions, women have come to mind. Single women, in particular, are likely to be rendered invisible and unheard at church. Pointing out that "churches and synagogues are family-oriented, with family suppers, couples' clubs, and children's religious education," Dorothy Payne observes that "too often we single people are seen as irrelevant or even threatening to this family togetherness."[3] Like any other group, single women are too heterogeneous to be described with a few generalized

---

1. Matthew 11:19 and Luke 7:34.
2. Gaillardetz, "Foreword," viii.
3. Payne, Singleness, 19.

words. They might be widowed, divorced, separated, or never married and still fall in the category of "single women." Nonetheless, they seem to share the invisibility of being relegated to the margins of today's Korean churches and the larger society.

As a never-married, single, female, Korean, ordained minister, my personal experiences at a few local Korean churches have led me to think that it would be hard for me to feel included at these churches if I were a layperson with the same status because their programs center around families and children. On top of this original hunch, I received confirmation regarding how invisible single women can be through a day-long conference for single women hosted by one of the Korean mega-churches in downtown Los Angeles. One of my friends who knows what my dissertation is about introduced me to the event after hearing about it during a Sunday service.

I contacted the pastor who was in charge of this event, and the pastor allowed me to participate in the event as a member. As I asked about the demographics of the participants, she told me that there would be divorced and widowed women, goose mothers (mothers of minor children whose husbands are living in Korea), and never-married single women. She was kind enough to assign me to a table for the never-married, where I could belong as a small group member. I was glad to know about this kind of movement in one of the Korean mega-churches. In fact, this kind of gathering was impossible years ago because single women themselves would have felt ashamed to be part of such a gathering. The looks from the whole congregation were not supportive or understanding. I was excited to attend this meeting, not only to meet other single women but also to learn what materials would be shared with these women at a Korean church gathering.

However, what I heard from the speaker throughout the entire morning kept making me question the nature of the gathering. I asked myself, "Am I really attending a single women's retreat?" When the speaker started his lecture by sharing about his family members, his lovely wife and three children, I felt the isolation and exclusion of single women worsen. His main goal of the morning session seemed to be to bring some healing through reminding the participants of the love of God, "the Father," based on a number of verbal and video examples he presented of the love of physical fathers, the roles of fathers in their children's lives, and the significance of fathers in all people's lives. He also constantly stressed the importance of being in a relationship.

INTRODUCTION

I was disappointed, outraged, and even offended by his insensitivity towards the particularity of his obvious audience: single women. The content of his lecture in itself was not bad. I think if I were a congregant sitting in a pew during a Sunday morning service, I might not feel the same way I felt, because I assume that more people would be able to relate to the message. As I listened to the guest speaker in this context, though, I thought about how these women would feel as they were reminded of their fatherless children and perhaps their husbandless predicament. Although I did not obtain what I hoped to gain through the event, his insensitivity or even ignorance has empowered me and reassured me about the invisibility of single women in Korean churches today.

As I looked back on the event, I realized that the guest speaker shared what he did with good intentions. I did not think that he presented his materials the way he did to harm these women. Instead, he must have intended to heal these women by putting an emphasis on the love of God the Father through an analogy of a physical father and the importance of having particular relationships in our lives. Nonetheless, I realized that good intentions are not enough when I remembered the saying, "The road to hell is paved with good intentions." When a good intention to help others arises within us, we ought to first put ourselves in the others' shoes.

Good intentions and putting oneself in another party's shoes, however, seem not to be the only necessary or sufficient conditions for guaranteeing the beneficial results that we intend. Although there might be a number of reasons for undesirable results despite good intentions, an epistemological limitation seems to have been a central element in the failure of the guest speaker at the single women's gathering. I am not sure whether or not the guest speaker ever tried to think about these single women's situational particularity. Let us suppose he did, because there is no doubt that he was there not to harm but to benefit these women in any way he could.

Even if he did, what made his audience invisible? As a married man, I assume that the guest speaker was not capable of imagining what it would be like to be a single woman in a married world. It might be beyond his capacity. Just like a person in Africa who has never seen snow would not be able to imagine exactly what snow would be like, this man was not able to really know his audience. The horizon of his understanding kept him from seeing who single women are and what they are going through. Given the fact that the majority of ministers of Protestant denominations are married men, the invisibility of single women has been a norm. No single woman has dared to demand to be known, proclaiming, "This is my story, this is my song."

The dominant discourses of marriage and family have unintentionally silenced single women's voices. Although I feel the need to advocate for all single women and goose mothers, they all deserve more than a book's length of attention to address their issues. Hence, I have narrowed down the scope of this study to never-married, Protestant, Korean-American, single women over 30 with a minimum of an undergraduate college education. The primary aim of this study is to develop an account of singlehood from the perspective of never-married, Protestant, Korean-American women giving voice to local knowledge that has been marginalized by the grand narrative of marriage and family promulgated by the Korean-American church. As a result, I hope this study will equip pastoral counselors to empower single women to resist the culturally dominant discourse by telling their own truths.

1.2. Discussion of the Issue

According to the creation story in the book of Genesis, in the beginning God created Adam and Eve to procreate so that humankind would continue on the earth. One of the creation stories indicates that everything created pleased God except Adam being alone. Since classical times, the Church has tended to teach that man and woman have been designed to be together from the beginning. I do not want to negate the significance of marriage or the power of family. Nor do I want to underestimate the magnitude of loneliness that can cause sleepless nights and a sense of isolation. In fact, I, as a never-married woman, hope to get married in the future. Nonetheless, I have found that a dominant theology stressing the value of family and marriage has been embedded within countless believers, thereby debilitating never-married single women's autonomy and prohibiting them from knowing their completeness in order to live their fullest lives.

A lot of never-married single women seem to be tacitly taught through their societies and cultures to consider their lives imperfect unless they get married. Dominantly embedded theologies stressing marriage and family have driven never-married single women to regard their lives before marriage as just preludes. The concert will not begin until the marriage is consummated. Thus, I think the traditionally dominant theology puts too much emphasis on marriage and family and is harmful to women who choose not to engage in a traditional marriage relationship. This theology has inadvertently played a debilitating role in never-married single women's lives, colluding with socially constructed negative stereotypes. Furthermore, the discourse of marriage and family has begotten the unintentional yet critical result of a "lack of sensitivity to the needs of single people" [4] and empty pews in churches. Compared to the support given to children, couples, and families in general, I observe a lack of pastoral strategies to empower never-married single women. The need for this study becomes clearer when the situation is illumined by current changes in demographics.

The never-married single group has notably grown. In part, this is because delaying marriage has become a trend in many parts of the world. Natalie Schwartzberg, Kathy Berliner, and Demaris Jacob point to the 1991 census report that shows "78 percent of men were unmarried at age 24, as opposed to only 53 percent single at age 24 in 1960. The rates for women unmarried at 24 have increased from 28 percent in 1960 to 61 percent in 1991."[5] A similar phenomenon has taken place in South Korea as well (see Figure 1). While the average age for a first marriage was 28.4 for males and 25.6 for females in 1991, it has become older since then, with the average age in 2013 for a first marriage being 32.6 for males and 30.4 for females. This trend means that more people have spent a substantial period of their life as singles. It is a twenty-first century phenomenon. Figure 1 shows how this phenomenon has manifested itself in South Korea.

I think the church needs to pay attention not only to this phenomenon but also to the demographic changes taking place in many developed countries in order to stay relevant to today's people. New wine requires new wineskins. Lucia Bequaert, in her book, *Single Women, Alone and Together*, written in 1976, observed that "young women between the ages of eighteen and thirty are simply not marrying—some 48 percent by some estimates."[6]

---

4. Schwartzberg, et al., *Single in a Married World*, 28.
5. Ibid., 5.
6. Bequaert, *Single Women, Alone and Together*, xi.

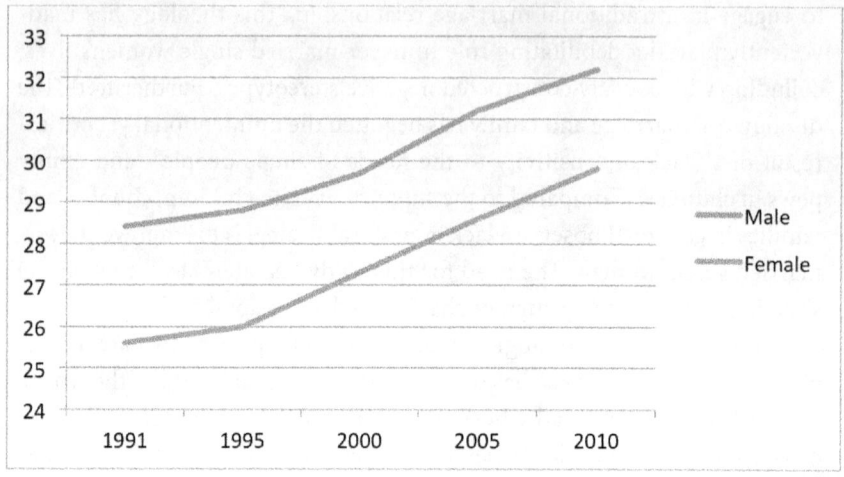

Figure 1. South Koreans' Average Age at First Marriage by Year[7]

Figures 2 and 3, from Albert Hsu's book, *Singles at the Crossroads: A Fresh Perspective on Christian Singleness*, well demonstrates the drastic changes in the population of U.S. adults during the twentieth century. The percentage of singles in the population in 1996—43 percent—was a considerable increase over the 5 percent of the U.S. population in 1900 that was single. It is not an exaggeration to estimate that now nearly half of the U.S. population is comprised of single adults. Hsu quotes Pamela Cytrynbaum's statement that "some experts predict that single adults will account for fully half of the adult population by the turn of the century."[8] The fulfillment of this prediction is well expressed through the subtitle of Kay Collier-Slone's book, *Single in the Church*, which is "New Ways to Minister with 52 percent of God's People."

---

7. "The Average Age for the First Marriage," The National Statistics Office, accessed April. 6, 2016, https://web.archive.org/web/*/http://stat.seoul.go.kr/jsp3/.

8. Cytrynbaum, "Today's Singles Are Looking for Match Made in Cyberspace," 14.

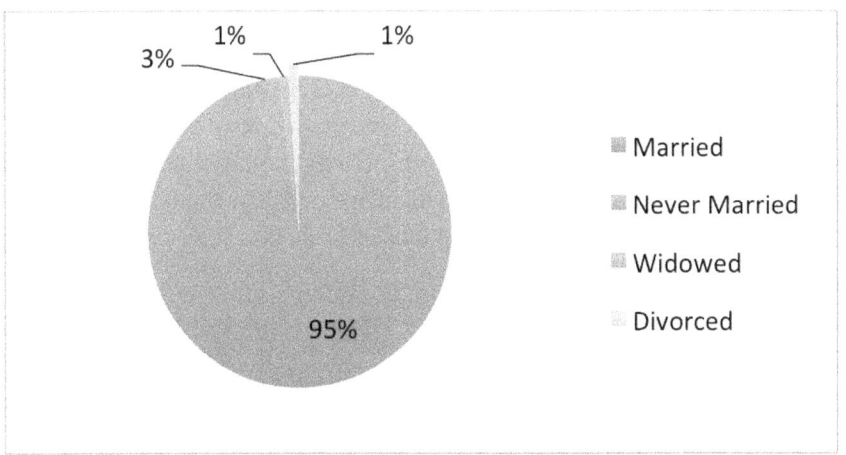

Figure 2. Population of U.S. Adults by Marital Status in 1900[9]

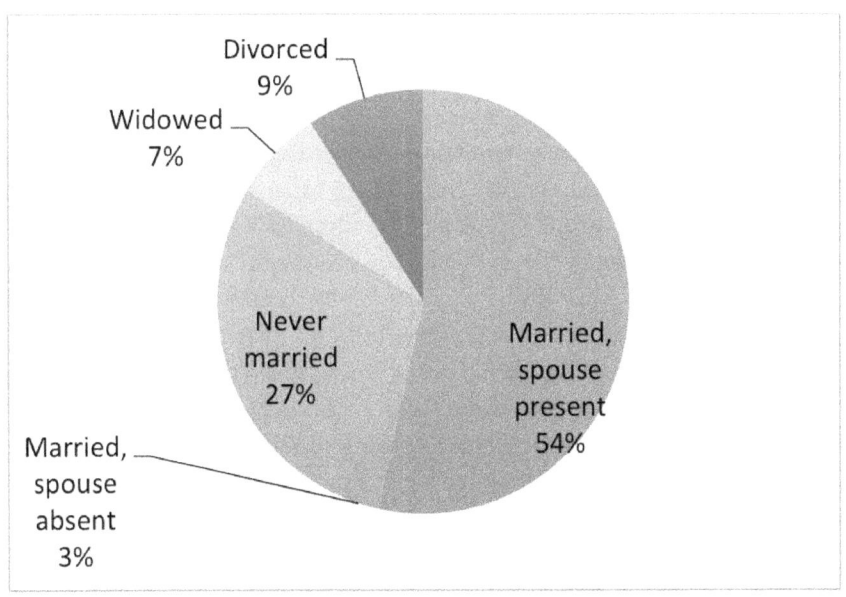

Figure 3. Population of U.S. Adults by Marital Status, March 1996[10]

9. Ibid., 15.
10. Ibid.

South Korean newspaper, *The Hankyoreh*, reports in an article titled, "Four Out of Ten are Never-Married Singles" that South Korea ranks first among The Organization for Economic Co-Operation and Development (OECD) countries for its never-married single rate.[11] Whereas OECD countries' average percentage of never-married single adults over age fifteen is 27.1 percent, South Korea's percentage is 38.6 percent, putting it just above the 38 percent rate of the Republic of Chile (see Figure 4).

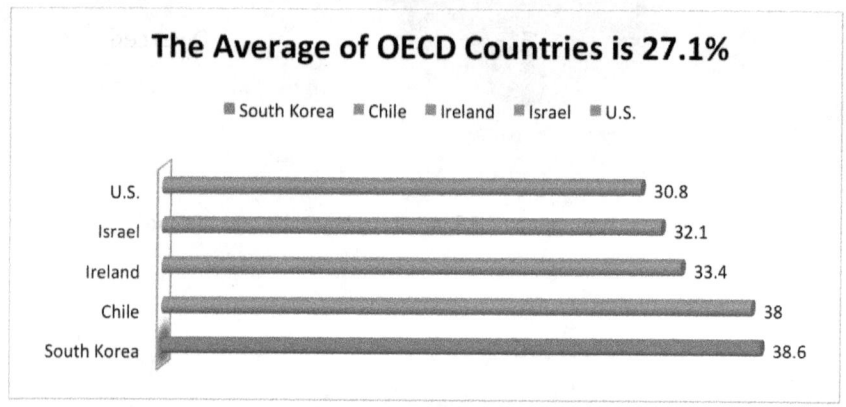

Figure 4. Average Percentage of Never-Married Singles over 15 (2012)[12]

In brief, more people in the past few decades have spent substantial periods of their adult lives as singles than ever before. The never-married single population constitutes a considerable percentage of the population not only in the U.S. and South Korea, but also in many other countries around the world. Nevertheless, I do not think this reflects the population of most local churches. Some lines from a sermon by David Johnson cited by Hsu support my hypothesis: "According to national surveys, in most churches, the single population is 15 percent. And the smaller the church, the less population of single people there are, because of this real focus on family and nothing else."[13] I agree with Johnson that the church does not have a place for never-married singles because of its theology that highlights the importance of family and marriage.

11. Park, "Four out of Ten are Single in South Korea: First Rank among OECD Countries," *The Hankyoreh*, May 6, 2014, https://web.archive.org/web/*/http://www.hani.co.kr/arti/society/society_general/635761.html.

12. Ibid.

13. Johnson, "The Pain of Porneia," 25.

In fact, the dominant embedded theology is not the only culprit in relegating never-married, single women to the margins. According to Debra Farrington, "Almost every adult development model created by psychologists assumes that adults are married."[14] Just like it is a natural developmental progress to enter junior high after elementary school, and high school after junior high, most popular developmental theories assume that all "normal" people get married at a certain point in their lives. The general social understanding of single adults and the response of their parents are well captured in the following passage from *Single in a Married World*:

> In addition to experiencing oneself as out of step with the wider society, the adult who remains single beyond the standard age range may also feel out of step with the norms of his or her own family.... Most families define the eventual marriage of the children as part of the natural evolution of the family. It can signal to parents that they have successfully reared their children to "mature adulthood," especially in the eyes of the surrounding culture.[15]

Since marriage is taken for granted, people tend to regard never-married singles as failures who have not been able to achieve one of life's major goals, thus deviating from the normal route for human beings.

According to Mary Dell, a psychiatrist, "Often a single woman is compelled to enter psychotherapy when messages she has internalized from her family of origin and traditional society have convinced her that she is a failure because she has not married, and that if she could only find and fix the flaws, she would be 'good enough' to attract a 'good enough' man and marry."[16] As members of society, it is not surprising that never-married, single women internalize these negative images, having been domesticated by the dominant discourse of marriage and family.

I will elaborate on the issue of the subjugation of the singlehood discourse in more detail in Chapter 5 in light of two postmodern approaches, discourse theory and social constructionism. In that chapter I will explain why I chose to engage with these two approaches. Some readers might wonder, "Why wait until Chapter 5 to provide this explanation?" I believe it is important for readers to first see and understand the whole forest called "postmodern pastoral care and counseling" before I introduce particular trees within this forest. In order to understand each tree within this forest,

---

14. Farrington, *One like Jesus*, xxi.
15. Schwartzberg, et al., *Single in a Married World*, 7.
16. Dell, "Will My Time Ever Come? On Being Single," 315.

it is a prerequisite to comprehend the general cultural shift from modernity to postmodernity. Therefore, in Chapter 2, I will explicate the term *postmodernity*, drawing on the definitions of Jean-François Lyotard and Michael Foucault and describing how this cultural shift has taken place in science, ethics, and theology.

1.3. The Audience of the Study

The audience that I would most like to reach is those ministers and seminarians who will be or are dealing with single women in their local church settings. This study will equip them to have more sensitivity towards single women by expanding their horizons of understanding. Although my study focuses on never-married, Korean-American women, I approach the issue of singleness as one of the silenced voices on the margins of church and society in general in order to eventually bring *shalom* to our whole community. Given the fact that "today the question of marginalization and oppression is becoming more complex and disputatious,"[17] pastoral care and counseling for the postmodern world needs to be sensitive to the subtle operations of domination and oppression in order to enable the church to embody Jesus' radical hospitality and God's justice.

---

17. Kang, "Theology from a Space Where Postcolonialism and Feminism Intersect," 61.

Chapter 2

From Modernity to Postmodernity

2.1. Introduction

THE SUBTITLE OF THE present study is, "Postmodern Pastoral Care and Counseling for Never-Married Single Women." The subtitle itself might lead my readers to pose a few questions, such as: Is postmodern pastoral care and counseling so different from modern or premodern approaches? How so? What constitutes postmodern pastoral care and counseling? Is not postmodernism something Christians should avoid? What does pastoral care and counseling have to do with postmodernity? What is postmodernism anyway? As the first step toward offering postmodern pastoral care and counseling for never-married single women, I would like to share a brief exposition of the epistemological trajectory from modernity to postmodernity. (I will interchangeably use *postmodernity* and *postmodernism* in this text.)

I begin with a broad understanding of postmodernity, drawing on Jean-François Lyotard and Michel Foucault because these two scholars' approaches speak most meaningfully to me as I build a conversation between postmodernism and the field of pastoral care and counseling for never-married women (reasons for this will be explained later). Then, I trace the trajectory of postmodernity in order to enhance my readers' understanding. To do this, I look at the concepts of objectivity and dualism. Lyotard understands postmodernism as incredulity toward big stories. This understanding fascinates me as a means to empower silenced voices to speak for themselves. Yet, it is an incomplete definition, as my critique below establishes. I will define the term in my own words, drawing from Foucault.

My purpose here, though, is not to review the whole development from modernity to postmodernity in detail (since it deserves a book all by itself), but to provide some philosophical foundations for my readers so that my readers and I share the same rules of the game. Through the lens of Wittgenstein's concept of a "language game," the current study will make more sense for those who understand my perspective on the rules of the game of postmodernity. I will specifically discuss how the ethos of objectivity has lost its grip in the academic realms of science, ethics, and theology. The alteration in the status of knowledge over time will be explained through a description of the emergence of a postmodern attitude as it eclipsed modernity. A more detailed explanation with respect to the trajectory of epistemological development from modernity to postmodernity will be added to help readers understand Lyotard's definition of *postmodern*, which I consider the cornerstone of postmodern thought.

2.2. Incredulity toward Big Stories

In *The Postmodern Condition: A Report on Knowledge,* Jean-François Lyotard explicitly defines this somewhat nebulous term. "Simplifying to the extreme, I define postmodern as incredulity toward metanarratives."[1] Given that the literal meaning of the word *metanarratives* is "big stories," *postmodernism* means suspicion of and distrust in big stories. I perceive disbelief in metanarratives as the core epistemological foundation that has awakened the dawn of postmodernity. In this vein, I find postmodern thought very appealing to the extent that it can be a profound means for empowering those whose voices have been silenced and marginalized.

The term *postmodernism*, stemming from Martin Heidegger's philosophy, was only beginning to enter the full range of the human sciences in the 1980s, despite the emergence of postmodern tendencies in a variety of philosophical orientations in the 1960s in the United States.[2] In fact, an initial turn from modernity to postmodernity began to surface at the end of the 1950s in Europe. Since the 1950s, the phenomena of postmodernity

---

1. Lyotard, *The Postmodern Condition*, xxiv.
2. Heidegger's first major work, *Being and Time* (1927), laid a philosophical foundation for postmodern thought, influencing writers such as Charles Olson, Alain Robbe-Grillet, and Susan Sontag.

have permeated every nook and cranny of the cultures of most Western developed countries, whether people are able to recognize these phenomena as postmodern or not.

For example, let us think about Columbus Day in the United States. Whereas people used to celebrate the discovery of a new continent by Columbus, a new voice has emerged that has questioned the meaning of this day. According to this new voice, what should be remembered on Columbus Day is not Columbus' victory but the sacrifice that the Native Americans were forced to make. In fact, this new voice has borne fruit in Seattle, resulting in a different name for Columbus Day. Reuters reported on October 6, 2014, that "the Seattle City Council unanimously voted . . . to redesignate the federal Columbus Day holiday as Indigenous People's Day to reflect that Native Americans were living on the continent before Christopher Columbus' fifteenth Century arrival."[3] It seems to be only a matter of time before Columbus Day fades into the mists of history.

This change in perspective regarding a national holiday is a sign of a postmodern turn, whether or not people identify it as postmodern. Indeed, the term *postmodernism* has inundated every aspect of today's societies, from the arts and music to literature, architecture, government, and so on. According to Patricia Waugh, "for over a decade, *postmodernism* has been a key term in the vocabularies not only of literary theorists but also political scientists, philosophers, geographers, media theorists and sociologists."[4] Postmodernism has become an important force shaping contemporary experience in and beyond the church, and pastoral care and counseling must take this into consideration. The imprint of postmodernity on today's world is actually immeasurable. In fact, the imprint reaches to theology as well, including care and counseling, as I will elaborate in Chapter 2 and 3.

For now, let us look into what the big stories are and why we need to distrust them. What Lyotard means by "metanarratives" is well articulated in his letter to Marthias Kahn titled, "Missive on Universal History," in the book *The Postmodern Explained*:

> . . . the Christian narrative of the redemption of original sin through love; the *Aufklärung* narrative of emancipation from

---

3. Victoria Cavaliere, "Seattle Lawmakers Vote to Change Name of Columbus Day Holiday," *Reuters*, October 6, 2014, available from https://web.archive.org/web/*/http://www.reuters.com/article/2014/10/06/us-usa-washington-columbus-idUSKCN0HV27E20141006?feedType=RSS&feedName=domesticNews.

4. Waugh, "Introduction," 1.

ignorance and servitude through knowledge and egalitarianism; the speculative narrative of the realization of the universal Idea through the dialectic of the concrete; the Marxist narrative of emancipation from exploitation and alienation through the socialization of work; and the capitalist narrative of emancipation from poverty through technoindustrial development.[5]

The primary narratives of Christianity, the Enlightenment, Speculative theories, Marxism, and Capitalism are the grand narratives that we need to distrust. In fact, these narratives have become scarcely credible because they fail to fulfill what they have promised: a better world for all.[6] Instead of a better world for all, these narratives have brought a better world for the few, resulting in totalitarianism and terror, with millions of victims.

What I want to put an emphasis on within Lyotard's analysis of postmodernism is that not all grand stories can become metanarratives. The grand narratives that we need to distrust are not only big stories in size, but their characteristic of claiming legitimacy by appealing to universality and universal reason in particular. In fact, James Smith puts it this way: "What is at stake for Lyotard is not the scope of these narratives but the nature of the claims they make. The problem isn't the stories they tell but the way they tell them (and, to a degree, why they tell them)."[7] In other words, modern scientific stories that assert their authority on a foundation of objectivity are what Lyotard meant by "metanarratives."

Lyotard's working hypothesis is that "the status of knowledge is altered as societies enter what is known as the postindustrial age and cultures enter what is known as the postmodern age."[8] Whereas scientific knowledge enjoyed absolute power in modernity, its status has been altered in the postmodern era. Claims to being "universal" and "objective" no longer have the authority to prove the legitimacy of many things, since there has been a cultural progression from modernity to postmodernity. Juxtaposing scientific knowledge with narrative knowledge, Lyotard emphasizes the importance of paying attention to the narrative aspect of knowledge in postmodernity (I will explain the narrative aspect of knowledge in chapter

---

5. Lyotard, *The Postmodern Explained*, 25.

6. Lyotard enumerates some historical evidences of these narratives' failure in the same article 28–29.

7. Smith, *Who's Afraid of Postmodernism?*, 64.

8. Lyotard, *The Postmodern Condition*, 3.

5) so as to bring "internal equilibrium and conviviality."[9] It seems to me that it is the balance between scientific knowledge and narrative knowledge that makes our knowledge more wholesome.

2.3. A Description of Postmodern

Given its nebulous character of being understood from various points of view in different disciplines, I want to articulate what I mean by the term *postmodern* for the current study before proceeding to the main discussion. As the term itself indicates with the prefix *post-*, a lot of people regard postmodernity as an epoch chronologically following modernity, albeit with a blurry demarcation. Although I do not have any objection to perceiving postmodernity in this way, for me the chronological understanding of postmodernity is less compelling than Michel Foucault's comprehension of it as a shift in attitude rather than in chronology.

Critiquing the envisagement of modernity on a timeline, Foucault encourages us to consider modernity as an attitude rather than a period of history. Foucault's approach seems applicable not only for modernity but for postmodernity and premodernity as well. His elaboration on the concept of "attitude" is as follows: "By 'attitude,' I mean a mode of relating to contemporary reality; a voluntary choice made by certain people; in the end, a way of thinking and feeling; a way, too, of acting and behaving."[10] Thus, for Foucault, "attitude" is a mode of thinking. In light of Foucault's understanding, it seems to me that "postmodernity" can be thought of as a new way of understanding the world, a worldview.

Namely, postmodernity is like a lens through which we perceive the world. Like a different color lens in my swimming goggles gives me a different view of the water in the swimming pool, our ways of perceiving the world will differ depending on the lenses we put on. In that sense, I think that Foucault's "attitude" can be likened to a map. That is, one's ways of understanding the world might not be tantamount to the way the world really is, just like a map is not the same as the real territory, despite the topographer's best intentions. Although people are not always aware of their own particular lenses, we do perceive through invisible lenses every time we interpret the world we experience.

---

9. Ibid., 7.
10. Foucault, "From What Is Enlightenment," 100.

Other people call this concept a "paradigm." Postmodernity is one paradigm, along with the lenses of premodernity and modernity, we can employ as we try to make sense of contemporary reality as well as the sacred. Interestingly, these three lenses can simultaneously coexist within a person. For example, pastoral caregivers can draw upon these three paradigms in any given caregiving context. In *The Practice of Pastoral Care: A Postmodern Approach* (2006), Carrie Doehring seamlessly shows, albeit briefly, how these three paradigms, which she calls "trifocal lenses," are harmoniously utilized as pastoral caregivers provide people in crisis with assistance.

Whereas a premodern lens can be used to "focus on the careseeker's religious and spiritual experiences of feeling connected to God or the sacred," caregivers can shift to using a modern lens to understand "biblical texts, theological problems like suffering, and the psychological experiences of acute stress."[11] Furthermore, a postmodern lens will enable caregivers to understand particular meanings and specific ways of connecting with the sacred that their careseekers have constructed based on the contextual and provisional nature of knowledge.

Although Doehring's book lacks a philosophical foundation commensurate with its subtitle, "a postmodern approach," I think Doehring's description of the trifocal lenses does a wonderful job of summarizing in a nutshell the epistemological trajectory from premodernity to modernity to postmodernity. Doehring's use of the term *knowledge* in lieu of *epistemology* also helps readers to be more easily attuned to this cultural shift. With a premodern lens, pastoral caregivers assume they can understand and experience a glimpse of the sacred through their religious texts, traditions, rituals, and so on. Modern caregivers employ more critical methods, such as biblical criticism and medical/psychological knowledge, in their efforts to approach the sacred and offer pastoral care.

Whereas the modern paradigm has employed critical tools to examine the sacred, it seems that the premodern and modern paradigms are similar in that they presuppose the sacred is simply out there waiting to be found. Indeed, "central to the modernist view was a robust commitment to an objective and knowable world, and the promise of truth about this world."[12] To the contrary, the postmodern paradigm has put an emphasis on the ambiguity of the sacred. No matter the critical tools human beings utilize to examine the sacred, people with a postmodern lens recognize the impos-

---

11. Doehring, *The Practice of Pastoral Care*, 2–3.
12. Gergen, *The Saturated Self*, 83.

sibility of fully comprehending exactly what the sacred is because human limitations keep us from such a full comprehension. Hence, a postmodern lens prevents caregivers from assuming an all-knowing and all-powerful role, since they acknowledge the limitations of their own experiences and knowledge, even in relation to God.

I think that people in the postmodern era have started comprehending reality, including the sacred, differently from people in the modern era, not because reality has changed, but because they are employing a different lens to look at and analyze it. In other words, the way they understand reality has altered based on changes in their epistemologies, i.e., their accounts of reality and knowledge. This shift is like looking in the magic mirrors at an amusement park that reflect people's outward appearances in various ways: taller, thinner, fatter, and so on. Just as my reflection differs based on the type of mirror onto which my figure is reflected, regardless of its sameness, it is the variance between the lenses of modernity and postmodernity that make a difference. The real, if it exists waiting to be found, perhaps remains the same. After all, our understandings of the real will diverge depending on what kinds of lenses or attitudes we take on.

2.4. The Confidence of Modernity

It is time to return to my initial question about some of the elements of the differences between the lenses of modernity and postmodernity. What made this epistemological trajectory from modernity to postmodernity possible? In the North Atlantic world—Europe and the United States—modernity developed throughout the twentieth century. It was propelled by the development of science, whose lineage can be traced to the Enlightenment, also called "the Age of Reason," in the middle of the seventeenth and eighteenth centuries. I consider the Enlightenment the beginning of modernity in that the capacity for reason and observation has been held in high regard since this period as a way to raise humankind from superstition and ignorance. The inherent connections between science, progress, and happiness used to be presupposed, not only during the Enlightenment period but also in modernity.

The father of Piscine Molitor Patel (called "Pi") in Yann Martel's novel, *Life of Pi*, reminds me of how the spirit of modernity resonated with Enlightenment thinkers' premises. While the protagonist, Pi, is interested in religions from an early age, his father, who believes in science, is concerned about Pi's efforts to be a Hindu, Christian, and Muslim at the same time. Pi's father says to his wife, "I don't understand it. We're a modern Indian family; we live in a modern way; India is on the cusp of becoming a truly modern and advanced nation—and here we've produced a son who thinks he's the reincarnation of Sri Ramakrishna."[13]

In Pi's father's eyes, his son's interreligious effort to be a Hindu, Christian, and Muslim appears useless in terms of bringing him success in a modern society. In fact, Pi's father seems to even perceive it as harmful to devote oneself to religions which are considered to be opposed to science. Out of concern, his father advises Pi, pointing out that "progress is unstoppable. It is the drumbeat to which we must all march. Technology helps and good ideas spread–these are two laws of nature. If you don't let technology help you, if you resist good ideas, you condemn yourself to dinosaurhood!"[14] In other words, any resistance against modern technological assistance will result in regression towards outdated ways of life.

As I consider the words of Pi's father, I can hear modernity's strong confidence in ceaseless progress. The belief of Pi's father in the novel is echoed in Kenneth Gergen's elucidation on what modernity is in *The Saturated Self*. In this book, Gergen comprehensively explains the shift from modernity to postmodernity in various areas, such as music, the arts, architecture, and even the concept of self. Identifying modernity with the phrase, "the grand narrative of progress," Gergen remarks that "the grand narrative is one of continuous upward movement–improvement, conquest, achievement– toward some goal."[15] What I understand by "some goal" is the building of a utopia into which the technological development brought about by science will eventually lead human beings. Blind trust in the grand narrative of progress ensured a certain credibility in the human capacities for reason and observation, including the ethos of objectivity. In fact, objectivity has gained prestige since the Enlightenment in the Mid-seventeenth century, along with rationality.

---

13. Martel, *Life of Pi*, 74.
14. Ibid., 74–75.
15. Gergen, *The Saturated Self*, 30.

2.5. Guarantor of Modern Confidence: The Ethos of Objectivity

The ethos of objectivity has a long philosophical tradition in dualism, which dates prior to beyond the Enlightenment. Plato is well recognized for his paradigm that divided the world into binary opposites: good vs. evil, soul vs. body, men vs. women, and rationality vs. subjectivity. Rationality is considered objective and superior to subjectivity. Plato's dualistic ideas were handed down to Aristotle and adopted by Judeo-Christian theology without much resistance. According to Gregory Riley, however, the roots of dualistic thinking can be traced back to as early as 600 BCE in Orphic mythology.[16] Riley views Orphism as the root of the dualism of body and soul, and its influence has been passed from generation to generation down to today's people through numerous philosophers.

Riley's assertion that Plato and Aristotle embraced this dualistic Orphic view is quite persuasive. Like Hegel's remark that "it is just as absurd to fancy that a philosophy can transcend its contemporary world as it is to fancy that an individual can overleap his own age,"[17] every philosopher is bound to his/her own concrete circumstances. Likewise, every philosophy is contextual. It is indeed the Orphic view that influenced Plato and Aristotle. Plato wrote, " . . . so long as we have the body, and the soul is contaminated by such an evil, we shall never attain completely what we desire, that is, the truth."[18] For Plato, the body is like a stumbling block that hinders the heavenly soul from attaining the truth. We can get a glimpse of this dualistic understanding through the Aristotelian definition of a human as a rational animal.

There is no doubt that the longstanding dualistic hierarchy between subjectivity and objectivity has been reinforced by the zeitgeist of both the Enlightenment and modernity. For me, René Descartes and Immanuel Kant are outstanding philosophers who have played a crucial role in buttressing the ethos of objectivity in the modern era. Known for the dictum, *cogito ergo sum*, which means, "I think, therefore I am," Descartes, the father of modern philosophy, identified human beings' core essence with the capability to think. As Descartes was exercising skepticism about the reality of

---

16. Riley, *The River of God*, 143–44.

17. Hegel, *Philosophy of Right*, 3.

18. Edwards, ed., *Body, Mind, and Death, Readings Selected, Edited, and Furnished with an Introductory Essay by Antony Flew*, 43.

everything in the world, he arrived at the one thing that was so certain that he could not deny it: he found himself doubting and thinking. Descartes' own words, from his *Metaphysical Meditations*, are as follows:

> I find here that thought is an attribute that belongs to me; it alone cannot be separated from me. I am, I exist, that is certain. But how often? Just when I think; for it might possibly be the case if I ceased entirely to think, that I should likewise cease altogether to exist.... I rightly conclude that my essence consists solely in the fact that I am a thinking thing (or a substance whose whole essence or nature is to think). And although possibly I possess a body with which I am very intimately conjoined, yet because, on the one side, I have a clear and distinct idea of myself inasmuch as I am only a thinking and unextended thing, and as, on the other, I possess a distinct idea of body, inasmuch as it is only an extended and unthinking thing, it is certain that this I (that is to say, my soul by which I am what I am), is entirely and absolutely distinct from my body and can exist without it.[19]

For Descartes, thinking is the most critical attribute of human beings. Thinking is superior to the body, an unthinking thing, to the extent that thinking determines who I am, regardless of my body. Thus, contrary to the unthinking body, thinking exists in the realm of the good and objective.

Like Descartes, Kant considered the ability to think as the core function of human beings. In his article, "What is Enlightenment?" Kant defines *enlightenment* as a human being's capacity to be liberated from her or his "self-incurred tutelage."[20] What Kant means by "tutelage" is human beings' inability to make use of their own understandings. In other words, it is very likely that human beings turn to an external guide instead of thinking by themselves: " . . . a book which understands for me, a pastor who has a conscience for me, a physician who decides my diet, and so forth . . . "[21] For Kant, human beings' unwillingness to think for themselves is a stumbling block for their growth.

In addition, this tutelage is "self-incurred" because it is humans themselves who allow external authorities to dictate every action they should do. They rely on external authorities not because they are forced to do so or they are lacking in understanding, but because they lack courage and the determination to exercise their own ability to think. As long as

19. Descartes, *Metaphysical Meditations*, 132.
20. Kant, "An Answer to the Question," 90.
21. Ibid., 91.

human beings remain dependent on external authorities, Kant assumes, they remain immature. Only when human beings can think for themselves can they come of age. It seems to me that Kant's emphasis on thinking for oneself resonates with Descartes' emphasis on objectivity. Descartes and Kant are harmonious insofar as the ability to reason is regarded by both as the most significant way human beings become human beings and reach maturity.

I have found that one of the consequences of this kind of dualistic thinking is a hierarchical dualism between reason and emotion that is pervasive among people in the United States and also South Korea. Rationality is sought as people try to avoid being "emotional." Whereas reason has been understood as something indispensable for a more civilized society, the importance and crucial role of emotion was not recognized until the late twentieth century. The raised status of emotion has been promoted through findings by scientists in the field of neuroscience, such as Joseph LeDoux, a neuroscientist at the Center for Neural Science at New York University, and Antonio Damasio, a professor of Neuroscience at the University of Southern California.

Pointing out cognitive science's biased tendency to focus on a part of the mind only having to do with thinking, reasoning, and intellect, LeDoux calls minds without emotions "souls on ice—cold, lifeless creatures devoid of any desire, fears, sorrows, pains, or pleasures."[22] Our intellect without emotions is like a half-truth. Damasio supports LeDoux's claim through his statement that "in recent years both neuroscience and cognitive neuroscience have finally endorsed emotion."[23] The long-held antagonism between reason and emotion has dissolved since technological advancements have allowed us to observe the relationship between our emotions and our physiology. Although there still is a long way to go to subvert the dualistic understanding between reason and emotion, the dichotomy of emotion versus reason has started dissipating as people realize the deeply interconnected relationship between reason and emotion.

According to H. Richard Niebuhr, reason is trusted so as "to bring order among anarchic ideas, to clear paths through the jungles of superstition and to induce many a plot of nature to yield fruit for human nourishment."[24] Within this paradigm, people have believed that reason

22. LeDoux, *The Emotional Brain*, 25.
23. Damasio, *The Feeling of What Happens*, 40.
24. Niebuhr, *The Meaning of Revelation*, 1.

will enable human beings to continuously progress, resulting in a utopia on earth. Further, being objective is possible and even desirable. Reality is somehow out there, external to humans, simply waiting to be discovered by objective and disinterested observers. It is only a matter of having the tools to discover reality as it is.

2.6. Erosion of the Ethos of Objectivity

The core of postmodernism is its reactionary element to "the grand narrative of modernism" that signifies the possibility of a science-based utopia within our grasp in the twentieth century, a utopia rooted in reason and objective observation.[25] However, the twentieth century saw the First and Second World Wars, the atomic bombing of Hiroshima and Nagasaki, and Auschwitz. In fact, for Lyotard, Auschwitz is "a paradigmatic name for the tragic 'incompletion' of modernity."[26] People's dreams of a utopia led by continual scientific progress, where all human beings could live happily ever after, was called into question.

People today are aware that more development does not inevitably correlate to only positive effects on human beings. Moreover, the ethos of objectivity has been challenged as people have been exposed to diverse opinions, ways of living, modes of thinking, and so on through the influences of globalization. John McLeod identifies postmodernity with globalization, along with reflexivity and the replacement of grand narratives with local knowledge.[27] I consider the repercussions of the larger phenomenon of globalization one of the main reasons for the unfulfilled dreams of modernity.

Today's world has become smaller and smaller. Technological advancement has brought the global world into a small village. People gain more information and travel farther in fewer hours. Air travel has become more accessible and affordable. The parameter of what people can do within a day has been ever expanded through train and air travel, fax machines, emails, smart phones, and so on. As a result, an event in one country no longer belongs to that country alone. A sense of interconnectedness with people in other countries has been heightened by the ripple effects of local events throughout the rest of the world.

25. Gergen, *The Saturated Self*, 30.
26. Lyotard, *The Postmodern Explaine*,18.
27. McLeod, *Narrative and Psychotherapy*, 21.

For example, when a financial crisis harshly hit the United States in 2008, it was not only American people who suffered. In fact, it began the global recession known as the "Global Financial Crisis" that lasted from 2008 through 2012 and affected many people around the world.[28] Like blocks interlocked in a wall, hardly any country exists in isolation in today's world. News that spreads throughout the globe via internet and other media like the speed of light has reinforced people's sense of interconnectedness in a way that was unfathomable just two or three decades ago.

Personally, I feel that I currently live in a totally different world from the world I knew just eleven years ago, in 2004, when I first came to the United States. At that time, it was not easy to communicate with my family in Korea. One of my monthly activities was to look for a cheap international phone card so I could talk to family members in Korea. This was the only way I was able to maintain a sense of connectedness with my family. But now I can call as often as I want free of charge wherever I have Wi-Fi access, and I can even see them through a camera while I am talking with them. I constantly exchange free text messages, not only with my family members in Korea, but with friends in other countries as well. The global world has literally become a small village through tremendous technological developments in numerous areas.

The implications of globalization that I have mentioned are critically germane to the collapse of the ethos of objectivity. Globalization has brought different people so close to one another that they realize the existence of other realities. Not only through migration but also through technological development, today's people have more opportunities to encounter "others." In addition, people have been exposed to others without even leaving their own hometowns and relatives. What I mean by "others" is totally different people in terms of ethnicity, religion, culture, and so on.

Gergen evaluates this exposure to others as the main cause that has shaken the foundation of modernity, saying that "it is precisely this exposure that undermines commitments to objectivity."[29] Whereas most people in the premodern era died in the same locale where they were born, never leaving that locale during their lifetimes and interacting only with people they had known for years, today, many people migrate to other cities and

---

28. Wikipedia, s.v. "Financial Crisis of 2007–2008," last modified April 6, 2016, https://web.archive.org/web/*/https://en.wikipedia.org/wiki/Financial_crisis_of_2007%E2%80%9308.

29. Gergen, *The Saturated Self*, 84.

even countries. Unless human beings encounter other realities, it is unlikely they will come to know that what they consider objective and universal might only be an opinion.

Considering the time when Korea was more homogenous than it is now, the demographics of South Korea have changed a lot because of the number of immigrants from other Southeast Asian countries as well as other continents. It has become inevitable not only for Korean people but for people around the world to encounter others, either in person or via media such as TV, Facebook, Instagram, and Twitter. I was impressed that one of my friends from Burma was very acquainted with Korean table etiquette through a few Korean dramas she used to watch. Today's people have more means to be exposed to other people.

As people get to know others, sometimes becoming friends with them, what happens is that we "begin to incorporate the dispositions of the varied others to whom we are exposed, we become capable of taking their positions, adopting their attitudes, talking their language, playing their roles."[30] Explaining the emergence of a self populated with others as one of the results of integrating others as part of who they are, Gergen points out that this process eventually promotes "a steadily accumulating sense of doubt in the objectivity of any position one holds."[31] People have started putting what they used to hold dearly close to their hearts into question.

In other words, people have realized the inevitability of the presence of different ways of life, including cultures and views based on differences between ethnic groups, economic classes, political groups, sexual orientations, ages, and so on. The erosion of the ethos of objectivity has crept in with the aspect of globalization I have described. Further, globalization has enabled today's people to see more by stepping out of their cultural, political, and economic boundaries. According to James Cone, "The only way people can enhance their vision of the universal is to break out of their cultural and political boxes and encounter another reality."[32] Unless human beings are exposed to others, their vision of universality remains parochial.

In retrospect, I can personally relate to Cone's assertion. When I finished the residency program of Clinical Pastoral Education (CPE) in 2010 at Mercy Medical Center in Rockville Centre, New York, what I shared with other committee members and other peers very much resembles Cone's

---

30. Ibid., 85.
31. Ibid.
32. Cone, *God of the Oppressed*, 49.

remark. I said something like, "the CPE process has empowered me to understand differences at a deeper level, helping me to come out of the little box from which I used to see the world." My experiences through CPE were truly enriching in that I was exposed to a variety people, getting to know them at a level that was more than skin deep. As I obtained an attitude of encountering others as "Thous" and not "its" by honoring the first and foremost rule of CPE—"not bringing an agenda to the patient room"—I could not help but open my eyes to the existence of other realities. This realization empowered me to overcome unavoidable prejudices that come with who I am and where I am from.

I am using "prejudices" in the Gadamerian sense. Hans-Georg Gadamer defines *prejudices* as "biases of our openness to the world."[33] He seeks a rightful status for the concept of prejudice through revealing its positive side. Prejudices are not necessarily unfair or flawed to the extent that our being-ness as humans entails prejudices one way or the other. Contrary to the meaning generally attached to the concept of prejudice, Gadamer insists that it is simply a condition whereby human beings experience something. Hence, modern science's claim about being unbiased and free of prejudice is senseless, because, even if we are seldom aware of it, whenever we try to understand something, prejudice always comes into play, no matter who we are.

I think prejudices are like the epistemological boxes that Cone referred to. Without being exposed to others, we might not know the possibility of the existence of competing realities. We might easily demonize or caricaturize other people's realities through abstractions. It is not easy for human beings to overcome their prejudices and biases. However, globalization has brought human beings to realize the inescapability of a multiplicity of opinions, cultures, and different ways of living. This realization has resulted in an enlargement of the horizons of our understanding. As our horizons of understanding are expanded, we can comprehend more things than we did before, not because more things have been added to the picture but because we have acquired the lenses to see things differently.

2.6.1. Science, Ethics, and Theology

Whereas a single voice, "the voice of objective truth," was able to prevail in modernity, in postmodernity, many silenced voices have subverted

---

33. Gadamer, "The Universality of the Hermeneutical Problem," 9.

universal truth claims and traditional authorities, thus eviscerating the ethos of objectivity and ushering in the understanding that "even the most honest and sincere people can only speak from their limited perspectives."[34] As the ethos of objectivity has lost its grip, a major paradigm shift has taken place in many disciplines. Here I will review changes in science, ethics, and theology in relation to the concept of objectivity.

2.6.1.1. SCIENCE

Undermining all preceding postulations about truth and order, postmodern tendencies have challenged the ethos of objectivity in the academy, beginning with science. Science had been known as an objective discipline in which human subjectivity, such as biases and prejudices, had no place. Science had been believed to be based on theories resulting from scientifically objective observations by neutrally disinterested observers, i.e., scientists. However, postmodernity's critiques did not pass over the seemingly ahistorical, objective discipline of science. Starting with Thomas Kuhn's work, *The Structure of Scientific Revolutions*, the ethos of objectivity in science has dissipated, putting scientists' absolute authority into question.

Lyotard resonates with Kuhn, asserting that "this doubt on the part of scientists must be taken into account as a major factor in evaluating the present and future status of scientific knowledge."[35] When the process of exteriorization of "knowers" takes place, scientific knowledge cuts a poor figure, losing its absolute authority to claim its throne as the rightful heir of authority. In other words, the positionality of scientists is deeply interrelated to what s/he has found. Suggesting a quite different concept of science, Kuhn has revealed the reality of sciences being deeply affected by scientists' paradigms and lenses of interpretation. The discipline of science is not as objective as it claims to be after all. Nor are scientists neutral or bias-free.

Conversely, the parameters of any research are determined by the values scientists learned in a particular scientific community. Norwood Hanson's work, *Patterns of Discovery*, sheds more light on Kuhn's view of the influence of a scientific community. In the chapter dealing with observation, Hanson introduces two astronomers, Johannes Kepler, a German, and Tycho Brahe, a Dane. Whereas Kepler believed it is the earth that moves, rotating around the sun, Brahe, who followed Ptolemy and

---

34. Gergen, "The Postmodern Adventure," 52.
35. Lyotard, *The Postmodern Condition*, 8.

Aristotle, regarded the earth as the fixed center of the universe. Imagining these two astronomers standing on a hill watching the dawn together, Hanson raises the question, "Do Kepler and Tycho see the same thing in the east at dawn?"[36]

What would they see? I think that Kepler and Brahe would see the same thing: the sun rising over the horizon. Yet, their interpretations of the same object being reflected on their retinas would be different because of their two different presuppositions. It is like how a doctor, a lawyer, and a mechanic would see different things at the scene of the same car accident based on their professional knowledges from their own trainings. Although both Kepler and Brahe were astronomers by profession, the ways they saw phenomena differed because they were trained differently in different communities. For this reason, Hanson considers seeing an experience. Claiming that it is people, not their eyes, that see, Hanson avers, "There is more to seeing than meets the eyeball."[37] We need to remember that there are scientific communities behind all scientific paradigms.

It is impossible to create and sustain any paradigm without a community. Revealing that "scientific objectivity is achieved through a coalition of subjectivities," Gergen explains, "A single scientist may proclaim a discovery, but before this discovery is allowed to count as fact, numerous other scientists will examine the evidence, repeat the research, or otherwise attempt to 'see for themselves.'"[38] When the scientist gains an agreement from a group of people, his/her discovery then becomes acknowledged as "objective."

Furthermore, when a scientist studies a theory, s/he learns not only about ideas but also about ways to see the world and ways to do things within a particular scientific community where a certain paradigm reigns. Therefore, scientific history is not a merely neutral development of accumulated facts. Rather, it is complicatedly intertwined and interplayed with its social, political, and cultural contexts. Kuhn points out that "history, if viewed as a repository for more than anecdote or chronology, could produce a decisive transformation in the image of science by which we are not possessed."[39] In other words, Kuhn enabled people to realize the sociopolitical locations of all sciences by situating many theories in their his-

---

36. Hanson, *Patterns of Discovery*, 5.
37. Ibid., 7.
38. Gergen, *The Saturated Self*, 84.
39. Kuhn, *The Structure of Scientific Revolutions*, 1.

tories. Kuhn started dismantling the notion of objectivity, the stronghold of natural science, by showing the inevitability of socio-political location affecting all scientific work. Kuhn's analysis has enabled people to acknowledge that even putatively objective natural sciences cannot be separated from their sociopolitical contexts.

2.6.1.2. Ethics

Science has not been the only discipline where the ethos of objectivity has been challenged as people have appropriated a lens of postmodernity. It is interesting to see a very similar shift has happened in the discipline of ethics. Pointing out "a strict interlinkage between the kind of language called science and the kind called ethics," Lyotard mentions that the ethos of objectivity has functioned as an authority in the discipline of ethics as much as in the natural sciences.[40] Not surprisingly, ethicists have started reconstructing the notion of ethics in the postmodern era as they have dismantled the ethos of objectivity. Morality and ethics are no longer considered fixed things. Rather, morality and ethics are ongoing activities that require a continuous examination.

As a discipline that investigates how people can best live their lives, ethics is about morals that have often been perceived as being grounded in unchangeable values and universally applicable beliefs across history and cultures. What is right and wrong for the whole of humanity appeared too obvious to discuss. Morality was not considered something that human beings could choose to shape, but was something that shaped people, constituting their lives.

The demarcation between "moral" and "immoral" was very clear within the modern paradigm of ethics, which sought "a foundation for morality that [would] free moral judgements from their dependence on historically contingent communities."[41] People in modernity understood that it is morality's detachment from a community that makes it more reliable and applicable for every human being, no matter what community s/he belongs to. According to modern ethics, subjectivism and relativism seemed incompatible with the discipline of ethics. With this frame of reference, it was easy for the modern systems of ethics to claim its universality and objectivity.

40. Lyotard, *The Postmodern Condition*, 8.
41. Hauerwas, *The Peaceable Kingdom*, 17.

Beginning with the publication of Alasdair MacIntyre's work, *After Virtue*, in 1981, however, the modern concept of ethics' universality has been attacked. Along with Stanley Hauerwas's work, *The Peaceable Kingdom* (1983), *After Virtue* precipitated a widespread paradigmatic shift in people's thinking about ethics in North America. Naming the modern systems of ethics the "Enlightenment Project," MacIntyre argues that "the project of providing a rational vindication of morality had decisively failed."[42] MacIntyre's thorough historical analysis of moral philosophers has enabled people to realize the unescapable interconnectedness of apparently impersonal moral principles with their historical contexts.

Critiquing "the persistently unhistorical treatment of moral philosophy by contemporary philosophers," MacIntyre points out that this kind of treatment of moral philosophy "leads to an abstraction of these writers from the cultural and social milieus in which they live and thought and so the history of their thought acquires a false independence from the rest of the culture."[43] If this is true, Aristotle ceases to be a part of his Athenian community. The Lutheran backgrounds of Kant and Kierkegaard and Hume's Presbyterian upbringing have no place in their moral principles. Just as every philosophy is developed by philosophers deeply rooted in their particular social contexts, ethicists are not separate from concrete social contexts, walking in the clouds. An ahistorical treatment of ethics leads to misunderstanding.

Since MacIntyre, ethicists' attention to the sociology of moral philosophies has proved how misleading it is to ignore "historical relativity and/or arbitrariness" in ethics.[44] Putting an emphasis on how a specific community's history and convictions impinge on the very nature and construction of ethics, Hauerwas avers that "there is no such thing as universal 'ethics.'"[45] Instead, he insists on denoting the social and historical character of every ethic with a qualifier, such as Christian, Jewish, Hindu, pragmatic, utilitarian, modern, premodern, and postmodern. The claim of universality for ethical norms and principles has lost its strong grip in the postmodern era.

Observing that "the majority of those who are designated as great thinkers with important moral ideas tend to be white, male, and Christian," Traci West warns people not to make the mistake of thinking these great

---

42. MacIntyre, *After Virtue*, 48.
43. Ibid., 11.
44. Hauerwas, *The Peaceable Kingdom*, 1.
45. Ibid., 17.

thinkers were "isolated islands of knowledge, removed from any community context."[46] This misconception has upheld false boundaries between great thinkers and their communities and other people with whom they interacted. As West attempts to create a Christian social ethics based on shared communal values, she invites community-based people to be her conversation partners, along with a historically respected individual thinker, Reinhold Niebuhr.

For *Disruptive Christian Ethics* (2006), West engaged in a series of community experiences with black women in Harlem who shared the same neighborhood with Niebuhr during the 1930s and 1940s in order to develop justice-oriented values for public practices, because what justice is can vary depending on one's culture, status, and power. West's attempt resonates with the title of *After Virtue*'s sequel, *Whose Justice? Which Rationality?* (1988). According to West, the best way to create public practices that maintain justice-oriented values is to rely on "sources of knowledge that cross these boundaries of culture, status, and power."[47] Although we strive for justice-oriented values, this does not necessarily guarantee the formation of universally applicable principles for all of humanity, since human subjectivity is indeed intrinsic to every ethical system.

2.6.1.3. Theology

Let us turn to the discipline of theology in relation to this epistemological shift grounded on the erosion of the ethos of objectivity and universality. I wonder how this epistemological shift has affected the field of theology, which deals with the eternal God? Can God's eternity be altered by a human lens? Has theology been affected by the paradigm shift from modernity to postmodernity? The answer is "yes," insofar as God's eternity has been investigated by human beings who are limited by time and history. It is not a matter of who or what God is. What matters most is what kinds of lenses we put on. Therefore, a shift in theology seems unavoidable as people look through different lenses to analyze God. In this sense, Ludwig Feuerbach's assertion that "theology is anthropology" sounds more reasonable to my ears.[48]

---

46. West, *Disruptive Christian Ethics*, 3.
47. Ibid., 4.
48. Feuerbach, *The Essence of Christianity*, 37.

Although theological discourses are inevitably bound to human beings' historical and political contexts, God-talkers' arbitrariness and self-interests have been hidden behind the curtain called the "eternal God." James Cone rightly avers that "Christian theology is human speech about God, it is always related to historical situations, and thus all of its assertions are culturally limited."[49] Ironically though, theology has been a discipline where the ethos of objectivity has had as much authority as it has had in science and ethics, in spite of human beings' dynamic involvement in the creation of theologies. In fact, the intimidating jargon of "science" has been a means to hide human beings' intrinsically subjective influences on theology.

According to liberation theologian Gustavo Gutiérrez, theology began to establish itself as a science in the twelfth century, despite its two classical functions as "wisdom" and "rational knowledge."[50] It is Thomas Aquinas who played an important role in making theology remain mainly an intellectual discipline by broadening Aristotle's definition of theology as a "subaltern science."[51] The sociology of theology has, however, come to light, starting with the liberation theology movement in Latin America in the 1950s.

Since then, the sociology of theology has been verified as numerous new voices, other than those of European-American white males, have added to the field of theology, developing black theology, feminist and womanist theologies, and so on. For the first time, Christian theology has been studied in South America, Asia, and Africa, bringing a lot of different perspectives based on these peoples' own experiences. As different perspectives have collided, it has enabled human beings to realize their finite limitations and come out of the little boxes within which they used to understand God.

Among the many voices, I think that feminist and womanist theologians' works have brought a sea change in the theological enterprise by challenging the unquestioned assumptions regarding the objectivity of academic scholarship. Men cannot speak for women. White men cannot speak for black men. By the same token, white women cannot speak for black women or women of any other race or ethnicity other than their own, because of their own blind spots grounded in who they are and where they

---

49. Ibid., 36.
50. Gutiérrez, *A Theology of Liberation*, 4.
51. *Summa Theologia*, I, q. 1 cited in Gutiérrez, 4.

come from. This is what Niebuhr means when he artfully remarks, "There is no such thing as disinterestedness in theology."[52]

Human beings are able to speak of God only from their own conceptual frameworks shaped by their sociopolitical, religious, and cultural interests. What people think about God cannot be distinguished from their locations in certain historical time periods and cultures. Considering that theology had primarily been a male-dominated field, specifically, dominated by educated, Eurocentric men, it is understandable that classical theology is faithful only to their experiences. Therefore, it was theology that maintained a false assumption about the inferiority of women. St. Jerome, one of the Latin Church Fathers, once regarded women as "the gate of the devil." Aristotle regarded women as "misbegotten men." Unfortunately, there were times when oppressive theological discourses against women were deemed universal, with people not having a clue about the God-talkers' limitations.

Under the scrutiny of feminist hermeneutics, however, the fact has come to light that classical theology is based not on universal human experience but on male experience. Women have started adding a different flavor to theological discourse based on their own experiences in variance from men's experiences. Although feminist/womanist theology is rooted in women's experiences, this does not mean these theologies exclude men's experiences. The oppressions of patriarchal systems and their damaging effects have had a great toll on all members of society, regardless of gender.

The following remarks from Rebecca Chopp describe well the damaging effects of patriarchy:

> Patriarchy is revealed not simply as a social arrangement nor as individual acts of cruelty toward women on the part of men but rather as a deep spiritual ordering that invades and spreads across the social order-through individual identity, to social practices, to lines of authority in institutions, to cultural images and representations.[53]

Consequently, feminist theologies are not merely aimed at liberating half of humanity. They are not only about women's experiences and their rights but also about dismantling the imbalance of power dynamics as well as stereotyped role limitations for men and women. When women's full humanity is achieved, men will be freer and will be able to acknowledge various

52. Niebuhr, *The Meaning of Revelation*, 18.
53. Chopp, *Saving Work*, 56.

dimensions of themselves and consider fulfilling roles for themselves other than provider.

Promoting human beings' experiences as the birthplace of theology through a contention that, "Human experience is the starting point and ending point of the hermeneutical circle,"[54] feminist theology challenges what many have often deemed overwhelming to challenge in the theological enterprise. Its attempts have started shifting boundaries of normativity in the theological enterprise. Contrary to the classical idea that considers human beings' lived experiences subjective and therefore inferior to objective science, Rosemary Ruether asserts feminist theology's capacity to make the sociology of theological knowledge visible by using women's experiences.

It is not possible for a theology to take a value-free scientific stance. One's values inevitably affect one's perspectives. Therefore, Carol Christ avers, "Scholarship that has been presented to us as objective, rational, analytical, dispassionate, disinterested, and true is rooted in the passion to honor, legitimate, and preserve elite male power."[55] Feminist analysis enables people to realize that what has been taught as objective could be merely the subjectivity of those in positions of power. Further, it lifts up the relegated position of human beings' lived experiences.

It is noteworthy that *Mujerista* theology arises out of the daily experiences of Hispanic women, denouncing any and all so-called objectivity. Just as womanist theology has emerged because of differences between white women's experiences and black women's experiences, there are areas that are not faithful to Hispanic women's experiences in feminist and womanist theologies. Ada Maria Isasi-Diaz maintains that what theologians should be claiming is not objectivity but responsibility for their own subjectivity.[56] For this reason, Isasi-Diaz regards self-disclosure as a starting point of every theology. Theologians need to tell people who they are before sharing what they see.

I think the fact that no single discipline is divorced from the sociology of knowledge illumines a perspective of which theologians need to be aware. When theologians seek responsibility for their own subjectivity, theology will better serve the mission of bringing the "kin-dom" of heaven down to this earth than when it pretends to be objective and universal,

---

54. Ruether, *Sexism and God-Talk*, 12.
55. Christ, *Rebirth of the Goddess*, 34.
56. Isasi-Díaz, *Mujerista Theology*, 77.

silencing many other voices.[57] Current thinkers in interpretive social science and the sociology of knowledge have analyzed how philosophically impossible and politically dangerous it is to insist on researchers' objectivity/neutrality. It is philosophically impossible because to be human means to exist in a particular cultural context. It is politically dangerous because it can provide a supposedly legitimate façade that maintains the status quo and privileges those who are in positions of power.

According to Smith, "Postmodernism can be understood as the erosion of confidence in the rational as sole guarantor and deliverer of truth, coupled with a deep suspicion of science—particularly modern science's pretentious claims to an ultimate theory of everything."[58] As cultures have developed and progressed from modernity to postmodernity, the ethos of objectivity has been challenged and it has resulted in a change in the status of knowledge. What was once considered absolute and universal under the name of "science" is under scrutiny in today's postmodern world.

The universalizing of particularities has silenced a lot of different voices, resulting in a totalitarian viewpoint. This is the reason for another definition of *postmodernity* from Lyotard, which is, "war on totality."[59] With this paradigm shift in mind, I would like to review what has happened in the field of pastoral care and counseling. The next chapter explores the influence of postmodernity on this field. In addition, it examines the literature dealing with singlehood in light of this paradigm shift.

---

57. I intentionally employ the term *kin-dom* in lieu of the commonly-used word, *kingdom*, drawing on Isasi-Diaz's critique of *kingdom* as presupposing a male king. A detailed explanation of the term *kin-dom* will be provided in chapter 7.

58. Smith, *Who's Afraid of Postmodernism*, 62.

59. Lyotard, *The Postmodern Explained*, 16.

CHAPTER 3

The Influence of Postmodernity on the Field of Pastoral Care and Counseling

3.1. Shifts within the Field of Pastoral Care and Counseling

SINCE THE FIELD OF pastoral care and counseling is one of the divisions of the enterprise of theology, it seems reasonable to expect that a postmodern paradigm shift has occurred in that field. In fact, three stages of paradigmatic shifts have taken place in the field: from a classical to a clinical pastoral and then to a communal/contextual paradigm.[1] The field has engaged with various disciplines in order to elucidate a plethora of complexities surrounding human beings. Specifically, feminist/womanist voices in the field have made substantial contributions to enriching the field. The intercultural paradigm has merged to meet the demands of cultural pluralism around the world.

With the clinical paradigm reflecting a modern view, I perceive a postmodern turn starting with the communal/contextual paradigm, which was enlarged by feminist/womanist perspectives and the intercultural paradigm later on. The clinical paradigm was predominant during the early twentieth century, when the field was in its fledgling phase as an academic discipline. Considering the social situation where the popularity of psychology in American society began with Freud's lecture at Clark University

---

1. Patton, *Pastoral Care in Context*, 4.

in Worcester, Massachusetts in 1909, a dialogue between the field of pastoral care and counseling and psychology seems to have been inevitable.

While pastoral care within the classical paradigm was primarily understood in relation to remedying sin, this paradigm for pastoral care was expanded as the field engaged with wisdom from psychology and medicine to develop a ministry of healing by the late 1900s. Although a number of churches resisted the wave of modernism in theological curricula because it seemed to jeopardize the role of supernatural revelation and the unique authority of the Christian position, the resistance of churches could not stop the evolvement of the pastoral care field's methodological focus from the classical paradigm to the clinical paradigm. The conflict between theology and psychology in this period is well described by Paul Johnson:

> The conflict of theology with psychology intensified during the years when psychology was enjoying a crescendo of influence in the modern world. . . . the theologians are by this time vying with each other to employ psychology as an auxiliary science, to understand the nature of man.[2]

Although there were some people who criticized the field for its seemingly excessive attention to psychology, Paul Tillich's correlational method enabled pastoral theologians to move forward in terms of the relationship between theology and psychology. In fact, Tillich's correlational theory, David Tracy's revised critical correlational theory, and process theology enabled pastoral theologians to argue that psychology and theology could enrich each other without either losing its own uniqueness.

Compared to the classical paradigm, which considered confession and penance methods for "cure of soul,"[3] the clinical paradigm enabled ministers to understand the depth of human beings' problems in a broader sense by putting an emphasis on basic listening skills and empathy. Although the field has benefitted a lot from the clinical paradigm, pastoral theologians have realized the limitations of this paradigm in that its focus is very individualistic. Care perceived primarily as individual counseling has failed to conceptualize individuals' problems within larger social contexts. As a result, such care has asked troubled people to adjust to structural injustices rather than empowering them to challenge "systems of power, authority,

---

2. Johnson, "Pastoral Psychology in the Christian Community," 17–18.
3. Holifield, *A History of Pastoral Care in America*, 15.

and domination that continue to violate, terrorize, and systemically destroy individuals and communities."[4]

Further, the clinical pastoral paradigm gives too much authority to ministers as experts over their congregants' problems. Being influenced by mainstream psychological theories that consistently portray psychology as a purely objective science transcending the politics and culture of its era, ministers are understood as neutral observers who can diagnosis without bias those who seek their help. While ministers are deemed to be professional healers, congregants who come for help are conceived as being dysfunctional. Recognizing that "pastoral counseling is not a private practice but a ministry authorized by a community of faith," John Patton expounds on the importance of retrieving a caring community where caring responsibilities do not solely fall upon ministers.[5] A ministry of care needs to be egalitarian rather than hierarchical by including not only clergy but laity as well.

Furthermore, Patton upholds that "a central part of the ministry of pastoral care today is discerning the contexts most relevant for understanding a pastoral situation."[6] Beginning with Patton, an awareness of the essential interrelatedness of human beings within their contexts has compelled pastoral theologians to pay attention to various contextual elements, such as gender, power, age, politics, race, and ethnicity. The role of feminist and womanist pastoral theologians cannot be dismissed when it comes to the paradigmatic development of the field of pastoral care and counseling. Specifically, feminist/womanist perspectives have promoted postmodern tendencies within the field, stressing the true meaning of human beings' lived experiences as fertile sources of theological reflection.

Feminist/womanist scholars have long claimed lived experiences as essential loci for the work of the Spirit. Challenging the ethos of objectivity, feminist scholars have brought attention to the importance of human lived experiences, as well as feminist scholars' epistemological limitations, because of their own experiences rooted in their locations. The stress on women's lived experiences has contributed to reconstructing the field of pastoral care and counseling. Recognizing that "communalization and contextualization are no longer optional in the theory and practice of effective

---

4. Miller-McLemore, "The Living Human Web," 16.
5. Patton, *Pastoral Care in Context*, 216.
6. Ibid., 40.

pastoral theology, care, and counseling,"[7] feminist and womanist scholars in the field have broadened its horizons.

For example, Bonnie Miller-McLemore's image of the "living human web" has played a critical role, echoing one of the critiques of the clinical pastoral paradigm. Whereas Boisen's living human document drives people to seek individualistic healing and growth, the idea of the living human web helps people to see their problems as existing within interlocking social locations. Stating that "clinical problems, such as a woman recovering from a hysterectomy or a man addicted to drugs, are always situated within structures and ideologies of a wider public context and never purely interpersonal or intrapsychic,"[8] Miller-McLemore argues for the necessity to move from an individualistic focus to a wider cultural, social, and religious context. As the field has analyzed individuals' problems from a communal and contextual paradigm, it has confronted systems of domination that violate and systematically paralyze individuals and communities.

Further, feminist/womanist insights have played a particularly crucial role in expanding the communal/contextual paradigm by shedding light on the previously white, male-dominated field. With ardent attention to power dynamics, class, ethnicity, and gender, feminist/womanist pastoral theologians have empowered the field to play a prophetic and transformative role in challenging systems of power and authority. Emmanuel Lartey initially introduced the intercultural paradigm through his book *Pastoral Counseling in Inter-Cultural Perspective* in 1987. The intercultural paradigm reinforces the attention to the margins of the communal contextual paradigm by seeking to correct the problematic consequences of Eurocentric cultural, political, and economic hegemony.[9]

Referring to this paradigmatic shift, Larry Graham states, "The field has been awakened in a new way to the world composed of diverse communities, to neglected populations, to systems of justice, and to its white male middle-class liberal Protestant assumptions and technologies."[10] Attention to social dynamics, economics, gender, sexual orientation, ethnicity, and so forth has empowered the field to include perspectives from the margins. Insights from the social sciences, along with feminism, black liberation

---

7. Greider, et al., "Three Decades of Women Writing for Our Lives," 22.
8. Miller-McLemore, "Pastoral Theology as Public Theology," 51.
9. Ramsay, "A Time of Ferment and Redefinition," 12.
10. Graham, "From Relational Humanness to Relational Justice," 220.

theology, and process theology have enabled pastoral theologians to notice what individualistic care and counseling ignored.

Considering the paradigmatic development in the field of pastoral care and counseling, it is surprising that the literature regarding singlehood, single women in particular, has not reflected this developmental shift. Given the written period of the literature, it is understandable that it deals with the issue of singlehood from an individualistic perspective, spiritualizing it. Moreover, there has not been recent research on this topic in the field of pastoral care and counseling. To the contrary, the literature regarding never-married single women from other fields, such as psychology and sociology, reflect a more postmodern view than pastoral theology by trying to understand single women's lives by valuing their voices.

3.2. Literatures on Singleness

Despite some attention from the social sciences, the life passages of never-married singles have not been well researched. The subject has never attracted much serious attention, with the result being that understandings of never-married women have not initiated a significant impact on the larger society. Neither churches nor society as a whole are well acquainted with the lived experiences of never-married singles. Beginning in the 1970s, the literature notes the paucity of information of never-married single women, yet few researchers seem to have responded to this critique. As I have pondered why so little research has been done, discourse theory provided some clues. I will explore discourse theory in chapter 5; for now, suffice to observe that it seems to reflect how few never-married single women have been in a power position to write, speak and be heard, thus influencing the field of pastoral care and counseling. This absence indicates an evident asymmetry of power between married and never-married single women.

Referring to the dearth of social scientific literature on singleness, Lawrence Riley points out the absence of "a nomenclature with which to conceptualize the status of persons who never marry."[11] Riley considers the term *singlehood* awkward. Lucia Bequaert also indicates that "there are many studies of divorce, relatively few about widowhood, and almost nothing about women who have never-married."[12] Echoing Bequaert, Margaret Adams contrasts the relatively scarce attention to singleness to the spotlight

---

11. Riley, "Factors Associated with Singlehood," 533.
12. Bequaert, *Single Women, Alone and Together*, xiii.

glare of critical scrutiny on marriage.[13] Although 40 years have passed since Bequaert's book, *Single Women, Alone and Together* (1976), and Adams' study, *Single Blessedness: Observations on the Single Status in Married Society* (1976), not many changes have taken place in work done on single women. Contemporary authors continue to point out the lack of academic research on never-married women.

Hence, it is still true that never-married single women have been given very little attention besides some interest in how to meet "Mr. Right." In addition, what attention is given to never-married women in the literature is so problem-centered that it reinforces the negative factors of single life for women. For example, literature dealing with the issue of low self-esteem and loneliness of never-married single women as substantial problems without analyzing it as a socially constructed idea underpins the sociocultural stereotyping of never-married single women. For this reason, Luther G. Baker's article, "The Personal and Social Adjustment of the Never-Married Woman" feels like an oasis in the midst of the barren land. I find great value that Baker's claim challenges the social conventions about never-married single women. Although the article was written in 1968, Baker's assertion does not sound out-of-date at all. To the contrary, I admire his extraordinary call to dismantle "certain contemporary stereotypes picturing the never-married woman as deficient in personal and social adjustment and insisting that marriage and motherhood are essential to feminine fulfillment."[14]

Through a comparison between 38 never-married women and 38 married women, Baker's study supports the claim that never-married women may maintain a healthy and happy life, achieving a satisfactory personality integration, without a husband and children. This study demonstrates that marriage and bearing children are not the only ways for women to obtain personal fulfillment. Rather, Baker proves that women's functioning as human beings overrides their biological functioning when it comes to their sense of personal worth.[15] It is their creative contributions to society that provide them with feelings of personal worth. Careful analysis of never-married women's lived experiences evokes the realization that assumptions about never-married women are not true.

---

13. Adams, *Single Blessedness*, 3.
14. Baker, "The Personal and Social Adjustment of the Never-Married Woman," 473.
15. Ibid., 478.

More efforts to turn to women's lived experiences came to fruition through the publication of Adams' and Bequaert's books in 1976. Bequaert's *Single Women, Alone and Together* examined the lives of single women (widowed, separated, divorced, and never married): who they were, how they lived, and what they needed in light of the rising tide of the new feminism.[16] Adams' *Single Blessedness* shares a commonality with Bequaert's book in that they both addressed the issue of single women while incorporating a feminist perspective. In *Single Blessedness*, developed from her article, "The Single Woman in Today's Society: A Reappraisal" (1971), Adams elaborated on the benefits of being a single woman and the value of these benefits sociologically and psychologically, while also providing a feminist critique.

Challenging the unchallenged supremacy of married women over single women through demonstrating single women's sociological and psychological self-sufficiency, Adams strived to dismantle social discrimination toward and stigmatization of single women. Adams hoped her careful examination of single women's realities would prevent precipitous early marriages as well as throw new light on marriage. She aimed at creating "a wider and more flexible set of options that emancipate women from enslaving circumstances." [17] Although Adams' perspectives might sound too radical for some, I appreciate Adams' pioneering endeavors to take the status of single women seriously and try to offer alternative ways of being.

Single women's voices are also lifted up in *Single Women, Alone and Together*, published in the same year as Adams' *Single Blessedness*. It seems to me that the burgeoning feminist movement of the 1970s was one of the enabling forces bringing Adams, Baker, and Bequaert to value women's own voices. Bequaert addressed the issue of singleness based on the lived experiences of divorced, widowed, and never-married women. These voices counteracted long-held stereotypes about single women and shared a firm view of the value of singleness. Although these voices were mainly from well-educated, middle-class, White women, the works of Adams and Bequaert still make valuable points for empowering today's single women, regardless of their ethnicities.

It is unfortunate to see a great gulf between the late 1960s and the 1990s in the literature on never-married women, despite the insightful contributions of the aforementioned three authors. Married society seems

16. Bequaert, *Single Women*, ix.
17. Adams, *Single Blessedness*, 28.

to have failed to give attention to their endeavors, which could bring transformation to the broader society. Perhaps the epistemological horizon of the married majority is a stumbling block that keeps them from listening to the significance of single women's voices. The gap in the literature reminds me of how hard it is to bring about change in a society. It took almost 30 years for two more books about single women to be published in the field of psychology: *Flying Solo* (1994), by family therapists Carol Anderson, Susan Stewart, and Sona Dimidjian, and *Single in a Married World* (1995), by Schwartzberg, Berliner, and Jacob.

Flying Solo aimed to deconstruct negative stereotypes of single women between ages 40 and 45, privileging the voices of single women in midlife. One interview with a woman named Julia, which the three authors thought summed up the feelings of the women they interviewed, is worth paying attention to in order to subvert longstanding biases against single women. Julia shared,

> How do I feel about being single at this time in my life? I love it. I think it's great. For me at my age, this is like a whole new life starting. I am really having a lot of fun and part of that has to do with the fact that I am single. I wouldn't have that sense of renewal, of having a new opportunity to begin and make decisions for myself all over again, if I was in a marriage.[18]

Anderson, Stewart, and Dimidjian recapitulate the stories of the interviewees' midlife lives, noting that they express "a sense of freedom, adventure, self-satisfaction, ease, and an increased capacity to appreciate moments of joy and discovery."[19] It is affirming to know that these interviewees perceived midlife as a gift that led them to spiritual regeneration or transformation.

Single in a Married World (1995) is appreciated for its effort to reformulate a life cycle framework based on unmarried adults' stories. In opposition to the prevalent view that perceived singleness as abnormal, Schwartzberg, Berliner, and Jacob attempted to depathologize singleness, hoping to "enable single adults to experience their life as authentic in the present whether marriage is in the future or not."[20] Although this book is not solely about single women, I value this book in that it approaches the status of singlehood as a legitimate one and includes a wider range of voices beyond white, middle-class, single women. The three authors incor-

---

18. Anderson, et al., *Flying Solo*, 132.
19. Ibid., 325.
20. Schwartzberg, et al., *Single in a Married World*, 12.

porate not only single women's voices but also single men's voices as they reconstruct the life-cycle framework. In addition, I appreciate the integration of stories from gay and lesbian singles.

Although there is a still long way to go on the issue of singleness, I sense a paradigm shift through literature in the fields of psychology and sociology. In fact, it seems that it was a postmodern turn that stirred an initial interest in singleness in the 1960s. In light of postmodern tendencies to value diversity, the stifled voices of single women have finally obtained academic attention. Compared to the research on single women in other fields, it is surprising to find that there is still an evident lack of literature on singlehood in the field of pastoral care and counseling, despite the increasing need for such work.

This lack of literature seems to be one of the reasons that few churches are aware that single people want to feel included. John Landgraf's two books, *Creative Singlehood and Pastoral Care* (1982) and *Singling* (1990), along with Dorothy Payne's *Singleness* (1983), advocate that the single state is complete and fulfilling. *Living Alone* (1997), by Herbert Anderson and Freda Gardner offers positive alternatives to negative thinking about living alone. Although Anderson and Gardner deal with all single states—divorced/separated, widowed, and never married—*Living Alone* is primarily about the experience of living alone after the end of a marriage.

The sections on never-married singles are comparatively short in the other three books mentioned above, and they speak more truthfully to the divorced, separated, and widowed subgroups than those never married because of the authors' own experiences with divorce. In addition, given the outdated nature of all this literature, I find it necessary to study the issue of singleness from a new approach that takes into account contemporary people's lived experiences. In light of my feminist perspective, I found some shortcomings in the existing literature from the field of pastoral care and counseling that I have referenced.

Genuine care now means not only understanding the human document itself but also comprehending people's unavoidable embeddedness within intertwining webs of constructed meanings. Hence, the issues of singleness are never purely interpersonal or intrapsychic. Rather, they must be understood within the structures and ideologies of a wider public context.[21] Landgraf and Payne tend to comprehend singlehood from an individualistic psychological point of view. Spiritual and emotional aspects are

---

21. Miller-McLemore, "Pastoral Theology as Public Theology," 51.

emphasized. Upholding the idea that human beings can be happy regardless of their marital status, Landgraf points out that "the married state can be wonderfully fulfilling; so can the nonmarried state. Spousehood can be hellish; so can singlehood. . . . it can be easier to create a good singlehood than a good marriage, even in a culture that regards marriage as the better way to live."[22] Landgraf goes on to propose some attitudes and approaches that can help bring about a creative singlehood.

On the one hand, I am in agreement with Landgraf in that a person can be happy whether she is married or not, and cultivating a good singlehood is easier than building a happy marriage. On the other hand, though, it seems to me that his and Payne's solutions appear to treat symptoms while dismissing the sources of the symptoms. They are unaware of the essential interrelatedness of human beings within their contexts, such as the interactions of culture, gender, power, aging, politics, race, and ethnicity. Whereas Landgraf and Payne's approach seeks individualistic spiritual healing and growth for single people, I feel that Miller-McLemore's approach is more suitable for the issue of singlehood. The issue of singleness needs to be illuminated in light of wider cultural, social, and religious contexts.

---

22. Landgraf, *Creative Singlehood and Pastoral Care*, 22.

Chapter 4

Research Methods

4.1. Introduction

THIS CHAPTER DISCUSSES THE empirical method I employed for this study, qualitative interviewing, and Kathy Charmaz's coding techniques and the themes that emerged from those. The reasons why I chose a qualitative method for the current study will be illuminated through a description of the characteristics of qualitative research in relation to practical theology. Following that description, I will briefly explicate the qualitative research interview approach from a postmodern perspective, in contrast to a positivist understanding, using the metaphors of a miner and a traveler. The interrelated relationship between data construction and analysis will be presented. Drawing on Charmaz's coding techniques, I will give explanations of how the data was coded and analyzed and the common themes that emerged. Finally, I will address the issues of credibility and confidentiality, describe the co-constructors of the data, and discuss limitations and contributions of the current study.

4.2. Qualitative Research and Practical Theology

As I discussed in Chapter 2, the lens of postmodernity acknowledges that any perspective that human beings have cannot ever be purely objective. What we know is determined by how we know, and how we know is heavily dependent on our own socio-cultural and socio-economic contexts. We come to understand things not only through lessons in classrooms but through our lived experiences on personal and social levels. Thus, our epistemologies are always biased and value-laden, based on such aspects as our cultural, ethnic, experiential, socio-political, and religious backgrounds. The world in which we live or the reality that we face is understood and interpreted not as it is but through our conceptualization of it. Standing on this postmodern epistemological ground, I have been drawn to qualitative research, which presupposes "reality can never be fully apprehended, only approximately," and thus it corresponds to the postmodern epistemology that undergirds the current study.[1]

Just like a paradigm shift occurred in other disciplines from modernity to postmodernity, research methodologies have changed and evolved. In stark contrast to qualitative research, quantitative research holds the modern assumption that there is a reality out there to be studied and observed. Quantitative researchers usually write about their research in impersonal or third-person prose because their trainings have taught them to believe they can examine certain phenomena as objective observers within a value-free framework. As a result, quantitative researchers have tried to suggest universal norms based on "mathematical models, statistical tables, and graphs."[2] When sophisticated quantitative methods had gained dominance in the United States, sociologists Barney Glaser and Anselm Strauss pioneered a qualitative research movement in the field of social sciences with the publication of *The Discovery of Grounded Theory: Strategies for Qualitative Research* in 1967.

Despite widespread and increasing attention to qualitative research across the social sciences in the 1930s, Kathy Charmaz reports a major shift toward qualitative research by the mid-1960s, stating that, before this decade, "quantitative methodologists reigned over departments, journal editorial boards, and funding agencies."[3] For Ian Dey, Glaser and Strauss's move opened up new ways of thinking about social research based on their critical assessment of "armchair sociology."[4] Dey commends Glaser and Strauss for their valiant pioneering role in social science research. Countering dominant mid-century positivist methodological assumptions that stressed objectivity and generality, the arrival of Glaser and Strauss's book made quite a stir in its time, sparking "growing interest in qualitative

---

1. Denzin and Lincoln, "Introduction," 11.
2. Ibid., 12.
3. Charmaz, *Constructing Grounded Theory*, 6.
4. Dey, "Grounded Theory," 81.

methods beyond Chicago school sociologists and their students and subsequently chang[ing] the way American researchers learned these methods."[5]

Although quantitative research studies have made enormous contributions to the disciplines of sociology, anthropology, bio-medicine, and so on, the mistakenly perceived "objective" ways in which they have reached conclusions for all the people of the world have silenced marginalized people's perspectives and voices. Various methods of qualitative research have been utilized to lift up the voices of the silenced and marginalized. The following observation from Carol Gilligan rings true in the context of the current discussion of the shortcomings of quantitative research:

> The so-called objective position which Kohlberg and others espoused within the canon of traditional social science research was blind to the particularities of voice and the inevitable constructions that constitute point of view. However well-intentioned and provisionally useful it may have been, it was based on an inerrant neutrality which concealed power and falsified knowledge.[6]

In light of Lyotard's definition of postmodernity as distrust in big stories (discussed in Chapter 2), the contention of quantitative research that its validity is based on its objectivity or universality leads me to put quantitative research under the category of "metanarratives" and lean toward qualitative research, the purpose of which is not generalization. Qualitative research seeks to ensure a better understanding of little-known or marginalized situations through using "ethnographic prose, historical narratives, first-person accounts, still photographs, life histories, factionalized 'facts,' and biographical and autobiographical materials."[7] Qualitative researchers focus on providing their readers with as rich and thick a description of the situation as possible so their readers as well as they themselves can understand the world differently. Subsequently, the task of qualitative research is to bring about the advent of different actions based on more comprehensive understandings.

The purposes of this study are (1) to learn about the lived experiences of college-educated, Protestant, Korean-American, never-married, single women over 30 in order to lift up stifled local knowledge that could oppose the domineering grand narratives of marriage and family; (2) specifically, to learn about the ways in which these women have experienced

---

5. Charmaz, *Constructing Grounded Theory*, 7.
6. Gilligan, *In a Different Voice*, xviii.
7. Denzin and Lincoln, "Introduction," 12.

their churches' teachings regarding marriage and family as well as their ways of being and living in general; (3) to put these voices in conversation with existing literature and circulated stereotypes that have been socially constructed; and (4) to envision a form of postmodern pastoral care and counseling for this population that involves recovering God's justice and Jesus' radical hospitality in ecclesial communities. Considering that the aim of this study is to explore the lived experiences of Protestant, Korean-American, never-married, single women, I conclude that this study must be done from a qualitative research approach.

I consider qualitative research a powerful means to enhance my readers' epistemological horizons by exposing them to a competing reality, single women's lived experiences. Furthermore, through listening to these women's voices, I hope my readers recognize the unacknowledged violence that has been done to single women in congregations. Like Nelle Morton pointed out in a sermon that touched Rebecca Ann Parker, a new kind of listening and speaking brings forth a new kind of community.[8] Based on my conviction that when any one of us remains invisible, an aspect of God is also rendered invisible, I want to invite never-married single women's long-disregarded voices to the table of fellowship to share their truths. The church has to make an effort to listen to voices from the margins in order to bring the kin-dom of God down to this earth.

Further, I am inclined toward qualitative research because I am a practical theologian. Stephen Pattison and James Woodward define practical theology as "a place where religious belief, tradition and practice meets[sic] contemporary experiences, questions and actions and conducts a dialogue that is mutually enriching, intellectually critical, and practically transforming."[9] Thus, while the term *applied theology* connotes a simple application of theological truths and conclusions to practice, practical theology places an emphasis on more mutual and dialogical processes. Qualitative research methods are very relevant to practical theology because both disciplines have an explicit interest in specific situations and human practices.

John Swinton and Harriet Mowat explicate the possible areas of dialogue and integration between these two disciplines in *Practical Theology and Qualitative Research* (2006). Swinton and Mowat consider qualitative research "a useful tool of complexification which can enable practical

---

8. Brock and Parker, *Proverbs of Ashes*, 97.
9. Pattison and Woodward, *A Vision of Pastoral Theology*, 9, 7.

theologians to gain rich and deep insights into the nature of situations and the forms of practice that are performed within them."[10] As practical theologians endeavor to build bridges between theory and human experiences through cycles of action and reflection, methods of qualitative research will assist the processes of analysis of and reflection on complex situations. As a result, qualitative research will eventually achieve practical theology's aim not only to enhance apprehension of the world but also to ensure faithful and transforming changes. As a feminist practical theologian, I find great value in employing a qualitative research methodology as my research approach for lifting up never-married single women's voices in order to enhance the married majority's horizons of understanding and bring forth changes in our faith communities.

4.3. Construction of Data

I adopted interviewing as my method for data collection, relying on the epistemological conception of interviewing not as "a process of *knowledge collection*" but as "a process of *knowledge construction*."[11] In this sense, I understood the interview process in relation to analysis. That is, I did not think I was excavating some truths waiting to be found deep in my research partners through the interview process. Rather, I considered the process of interviewing a collaborative work designed to construct knowledge through questions and responses based on my research partners' lived experiences. Thus, this process is interrelated with analysis. I appreciate the seven key features of interview knowledge as "produced, relational, conversational, contextual, linguistic, narrative, and pragmatic" offered by Steinar Kvale and Svend Brinkmann in their co-authored book, *Interviews: Learning the Craft of Qualitative Research Interviewing* (2015).[12] These features well reflect the influence of a postmodern turn on the development of qualitative research interviewing. As I conducted 10 interviews over a five-month period, I worked with a postmodern, not a positivist, understanding of the interview process.

Kvale and Brinkmann contrast the understanding of interviews in a postmodern age with the perspective on interviews in a positivist era through the metaphors of a miner and a traveler. Whereas the positivist

---

10. Swinton and Mowat, *Practical Theology and Qualitative Research*, 72.
11. Kvale and Brinkmann, *InterViews*, 57.
12. Ibid., 63.

modern stance regards an interviewer as a miner who unearths buried objective knowledge that the miner cannot contaminate, a postmodern interviewer is understood as a traveler who "walks along with the local inhabitants, asking questions and encouraging them to tell their own stories of their lived world."[13] Furthermore, a postmodern interview approach acknowledges the interviewer-traveler's role in interpreting the original stories along the way. Hence, the understanding of interviewer as traveler recognizes the intertwined phases of knowledge construction through both the interview and its analysis.

Considering my role as an interviewer as that of a traveler, not a miner, I conducted 10 interviews in order to understand my research partners' lived experiences. I encouraged them to produce thick descriptions of their experiences of being never-married single women in their churches, work, and home lives. Each interview was audio-recorded using my phone. During the interviews, I took some notes to remember interviewees' body expressions. In addition, I took notes on research partners' facial expressions when there was a pause, remembering that "what participants do not say can be as telling as what they do say."[14] Along the way, I utilized a memo-writing technique as an "intermediate step" between data collection and writing drafts of my analysis.[15] Memo-writing took place in between transcribing and analyzing the interviews in order to summarize my thoughts and questions. Memos provided me with a space where I could make comparisons between data, between data and codes, and between codes of data and other codes. I found memo-writing helpful, especially for recording my thoughts and ideas about data.

Each time I returned from an interview, I wrote in a research journal about it. This was done not only to record every aspect of the process meticulously but also to encourage my own reflexivity. Through writing journal entries, I learned what I did well, what I missed, and how I would revise my interview questions for the next interview to engage with my research partners in a more open-ended manner. In fact, several of my questions were modified as my interview process proceeded. For example, I learned that not many never-married single women were able to easily respond to inquiries like, "Please share with me the ways in which church teachings about marriage and family affect you," or "Have you felt excluded in your

---

13. Ibid., 58.
14. Charmaz, *Constructing Grounded Theory*, 91.
15. Ibid., 162.

church community? If yes, please share specific occasions when you felt excluded." Without a theoretical framework, it seemed that it was not easy for the women to answer these questions.

In addition, I reflected on whether or not these questions might convey some negative connotations in the way they were framed. Thus, I tried to listen to the interviewees' more general experiences of their churches and personal lives. I learned to invite my interviewees to share their experiences at church by asking them simple questions like, "How is your church life?" "What kinds of church activities have you been engaged with and how did you feel about them?" And, "How do you relate to the Bible study in your young adult group?" Then I invited them to think about their answers in light of their singleness. Because of some common themes that emerged through the coding process of the initial interviews, I added questions such as, "How do significant people around you relate to your singleness?" And "How do you relate to sermons on Sundays?" I transcribed every interview before moving to the next one, except for the last four interviews. I tried to fully digest one interview before conducting another one, since recurrent revisiting of previous interviews was necessary to compare and contrast them with one another.

4.4. Coding and Analysis

Coding is a process that researchers use to "*define* what is happening in the data and begin to grapple with what it means."[16] It is more than a beginning in terms of its central role in forming an analytic framework from which researchers construct their analyses. For coding and analysis, I employed Charmaz's coding techniques articulated in *Constructing Grounded Theory* (2014): initial coding (line-by-line coding) and focused coding. I studied fragments of data line by line during the initial coding phase, and then I identified significant initial codes from among the numerous initial codes when I saw common themes that subsumed large batches of data; these became master codes.

As a tool for early analysis, line-by-line coding involves naming each line of written data. As I assigned possible meanings to each fragment of data, it was like interacting with my research partners over and over through their statements. Looking for what was happening in the data, I tried to understand research partners' views from their perspectives. By engaging

16. Ibid., 113.

in this process, line-by-line coding helped me see the data anew and engage with it in more detail. Line-by-line coding enabled me to perceive things that I did not see when I conducted the interviews and transcribed them. For example, my interview questions were designed to illuminate my participants' experiences in churches and their personal fulfillment in life. I hoped to place their lived experiences in conversation with existing literature as well as sociocultural biases. I did not think about the influence of people who were significant to my interviewees on their being single as professional women. Line-by-line coding helped me move out of my initial assumptions based on my own experiences. Whereas age 30 meant it was time to marry in my context, my interviewees' contexts seemed to tell them otherwise.

During focused coding, "the second major phase in coding," Charmaz recommends devising codes based on codes that appear more frequently or have more significance than other codes among the initial codes.[17] Thus, I followed this process as I identified my master codes. I used these codes to analyze, conceptualize, and synthesize large amounts of data. For example, one of the master codes, "social pressure," was formulated based on research partners' frequent remarks about the influence of family members and close friends on how they perceived their single status. I developed the code, "good women," based on research partners' desires to accommodate themselves to their future children and husbands while they pursued their professional jobs. Although it emerged over the last five interviewees' stories due to the revised questions I asked, this code was important to me because I found it significant to pay attention to and empower my research partners. Appendix D provides the master codes that I developed after studying and analyzing the initial and focused codes from the transcripts of the ten interviewees, along with emergent themes.

Charmaz finds value in focused coding in that "this type of coding condenses and sharpens what you have already done because it highlights what you find to be important in your emerging analysis."[18] Focused coding is where I discovered my active participation as a researcher in the construction and interpretation of data through my own hermeneutical lenses. I am the one who chose what to highlight and what to dismiss. I feel a lot of moral responsibility to interpret my data as truly as possible so that it is also perceived as true from my research partners' viewpoints. Of course, I

---

17. Ibid., 138.
18. Ibid.

was aware of the significance of ethical issues that are woven "through the entire process of an interview investigation . . . from the very start of an investigation and to the final report."[19] Nevertheless, I felt a more direct responsibility during the focused coding phase.

As I struggled with the pressure from this moral responsibility, Isasi-Diaz's insight that I discussed in Chapter 2 allowed me to have leeway to breathe. I concluded that what I sought in this study was to be responsible for my subjectivity instead of proposing an objective and universal view. Like Corbin's assertion that "doing qualitative research is a challenge that brings the whole self into the process," I acknowledge that I have been a part of the entire analytical process.[20] I appreciate Rita Nakashima Brock and Rebecca Ann Parker's coauthored book, *Proverbs of Ashes* (2001), because it models how to be responsible for one's subjectivity without "the shield of academic language, the screen of objectivity."[21] Their theology is powerful because it is based on their lived experiences. I do not want to wear the mask of objectivity, pretending I am a neutral observer. Rather, I acknowledge the hermeneutical lenses that I brought to this study.

I came to my research with experiences of having served Korean churches in New Jersey, New York, and California as a never-married single female ordained minister. In addition, my background in progressive theological education has informed how I viewed and interpreted the collected data. Feminist theory, social constructionism, and White and Epston's narrative approach to psychotherapy are the major hermeneutical methods that I drew on while I chose what to highlight among the numerous initial codes, and I engage with those in the following chapters. In Chapters 6 and 7, I incorporate my findings into the practice of re-authoring one's life as well as my vision for Christian communities. In the next section, I will discuss the emergent themes that arose out of the master codes.

4.5. Emergent Themes

I engaged in focused coding based on the common emergent themes found through line-by-line coding. According to Charmaz, focused coding means "concentrating on what your initial codes say and the comparisons you

---

19. Kvale and Brinkmann, *InterViews*, 85.
20. Corbin and Strauss, *Basics of Qualitative Research*, 13.
21. Brock and Parker, *Proverbs of Ashes*, 7.

make with and between them."²² In other words, focused coding is a process I was able to use to study and access my initial coding. As I compared initial codes with the data and studied them, I could see some repeated patterns. From those, I developed the following five themes: (1) a sense of exclusion from the women's own faith communities; (2) the importance of significant people's influences on my research partners' status of being single; (3) the research partners' overall satisfaction with their lives in contrast with prejudices against them; (4) willingness to sacrifice themselves; and (5) a desire for partnership and offspring.

4.6. Credibility

Regarding my acknowledgement of the active participation of myself in the process of analysis, some might raise the question of the validity of this study: How accurately have I extracted truths from the data for the phenomena studied? On one hand, I understand this concern. On the other hand, I want to remind those who raise this question of the constructionist foundation on which this study is grounded. This foundation rejects the positivist assumption beneath this kind of question. On this note, Corbin expresses her uneasiness with using the terms *validity* and *reliability* in relation to qualitative research because she thinks "these terms carry with them too many quantitative implications."²³ Hence, Corbin holds that the term "credibility" is more appropriate for qualitative research.

What Corbin means by "credibility" is that "findings are trustworthy and believable in that they reflect participants', researchers', and readers' experiences with a phenomenon but at the same time the explanation is only one of many . . . 'plausible' interpretations possible from data."²⁴ Agreeing with Corbin, I use the term *credibility* instead of *validity*. I acknowledge the role of my biases and pre-understandings in the process of my analysis. I think, however, these will not occlude my research partners' understandings. Rather, my past experiences have played a role in enabling me to step into my research partners' horizons of understanding.

Further, I spent about four weeks in a peer debriefing that exposed my questions and process to a disinterested third party, Dr. Samuel Lee, to keep my inquiry more truthful. Lee assisted me in sharpening my questions as I

22. Charmaz, *Constructing Grounded Theory*, 140.
23. Corbin and Strauss, *Basics of Qualitative Research*, 301.
24. Ibid., 302.

proceeded with further interviews. Although I did not have an opportunity to verify my findings with my interviewees before finalizing them due to time restrictions, I plan to send the final copy of my dissertation to my interviewees. If there are suggestions, I will reflect those in my further work. I present the findings of this study as not the only truths but as some possible interpretations in my effort to honor my research partners' perspectives and stories and my limitations.

4.7. Co-Constructors of the Data

As an interactive social encounter, an interview takes place between an interviewer and an interviewee. The interviewer usually asks some questions and the interviewee responds. When it comes to interview practices, Tim Rapley says a "bad" practice happens when there is "a hierarchical, asymmetrical (and patriarchal) relationship in which the interviewee is treated as a research 'object.'"[25] The interviewee should be treated not as an object for study but as another human being. Given the inevitable asymmetries of power and knowledge between research partners and a researcher, it cannot be stressed enough that a researcher needs to be aware of her own views so she can remain open and sensitive to what research partners share and not impose her preconceived views upon her research partners. Researchers' openness to empirical data is very important in order to not apply preconceived ideas onto the data. Remembering this basic guideline, I tried to present to my research partners an embodied sensitivity so I could listen to their unspoken words and any discomfort they may have felt during the interview process. Further, I have tried to consider my research partners not as subjects of my observation or investigation. Rather, I understand them as co-constructors of the data for my research.

To recruit participants, I contacted via email or phone a few acquaintances that have connections with this population, as well as senior pastors and other staff members at a number of churches in the Los Angeles area. I explained this study and asked these persons to share my recruiting announcement. (See Appendices A and B for the sample emails that were sent.) I asked those who made the recruiting announcements to emphasize the participants' freedom of choice. I wanted congregants and all prospective participants to know they had a choice and that their participation was entirely voluntary. Each individual was given the informed consent

25. Rapley, "Interviews," 19.

form (See Appendix C) before she participated in an interview. In seeking informed consent, I took extra care to make sure the volunteer did not feel obligated to participate; I informed each volunteer that she was free to decline participating for any number of reasons, and I did not pressure anyone to participate. I explained every step without any jargon in a slow fashion so as not to intimidate participants in any way. Also, I was mindful of my facial expressions so that I did not convey disappointment, which can be a subtle form of manipulation.

I recruited 10 Protestant, Korean-American, never-married, single women over 30 with a minimum of a college education from the Los Angeles area. With each one, I conducted a semi-structured interview lasting about one hour. I did not interview my close friends so as to avoid the dangers of dual relationships and further complications with analysis. My research partners' ages ranged from 30 to 42. Although I tried to find never-married single woman over 50 in Korean churches, I was unable to find any. The single women over 50 that I found were either divorced or widowed. When I discussed this struggle with Dr. Duane Bidwell, my advisor, he encouraged me to be satisfied with my current data, stating, "Even if you find one, she cannot represent all never-married single women in their fifties." His feedback once more reminded me that the goal of qualitative research is not generalization but shedding light on the experiences of an understudied group or phenomenon.

Three of my research partners immigrated to the United States with their families when they were elementary school students and have lived in this country more than 15 years. Six have spent between 6 to 10 years in the United States. Shannon (42) is the most recent émigré; she came to the United States about one year before this study for higher education reasons. All of the participants are attending Korean Protestant churches. Three of the women are students at the graduate level (one is working on a master's degree, and two are Ph.D. students); the other seven women are working professionals, including a registered nurse, a pharmacist, a lawyer, small business owners, and employees of companies. Confidentiality

4.8. Confidentiality

I have protected the identity of each research partner by using a pseudonym for each one and interchanging their job titles among them. I did not reveal their real names under any circumstances, except to use their initials during the transcribing process on the hard drive of my laptop. No identifiable information for my research partners is included. All information was kept safe from others' access. The primary data was erased from both my computer and my phone upon submission of the final draft of my dissertation in March, 2016.

4.9. Limitations and Contributions

Since the study was designed to explore the experiences of Korean American, never-married, single women over 30 with a minimum of a college education, this research does not include any single men of a similar age or background. Although I assume that not many Korean churches are aware of single people's presence as they plan events, I cannot make a definite claim that all women sharing similar social locations with my interviewees will resonate with the findings based on my interviewees' lived experiences because there may be some churches that make an effort to address the particularities of never-married single populations. In addition, given that this study is limited to never-married single women whose educational levels are pretty high and are living with economic independence, this study cannot speak for those women who are from other social locations.

Nevertheless, this study is unique in its effort to dismantle the dominance of the marriage and family discourse through listening to Korean, never-married, single women's long-disregarded lived experiences as competing realities. I believe this study will enhance married ministers' horizons of understanding so they recognize the experiences of marginalization my research partners have undergone. This study will provide insight to ministers who hope to build inclusive Christian communities where all individuals are accepted as they are through the embodiment of Jesus' radical hospitality.

CHAPTER 5

Pastoral Care and Counseling and Postmodernism

5.1. Introduction

IN MANY PARTS OF the world today, the modern way of understanding knowledge as universal and objective has been eclipsed by the postmodern comprehension of knowledge as "multiple, fragmentary, context-dependent, and local."[1] I do not think that the field of pastoral care and counseling is immune to such a shift. Rather, the field needs to find ways to respond to what this epistemological change means for practices of care. In fact, several pastoral theologians, such as David Augsburger (1986), Brita Gill-Austern (1995), Bonnie Miller-McLemore (1996), Christine Neuger (2001), Karen Scheib (2004), and Carrie Doehring (2006), have engaged with several key characteristics of postmodernity, acknowledging "the inevitably partial, particular, and political character of all knowing."[2] In particular, Elaine Graham's *Transforming Practice: Pastoral Theology in an Age of Uncertainty* (1996) and John Reader's *Reconstructing Practical Theology: The Impact of Globalization* (2008) explicitly deal with the issue of postmodernity within the field of pastoral care and counseling.

Stressing that "faithful Christian practice can only be effective and relevant if it takes seriously the challenges of the contemporary world,"

---

1. Hare-Mustin, "Discourses in the Mirrored Room," 19. Haren-Mustin gives a credit for these adjectives for postmodern comprehension of knowledge to Foucault and Lyotard.

2. Ramsay, "A Time of Ferment and Redefinition," 13.

Graham asserts the necessity of engaging with postmodernity for the reconstruction of Christian practices.[3] Given that the postmodern epistemological shift has saturated many areas of people's lives, I can imagine the postmodern lenses that congregants wear to interpret their lives. I do not mean to say that today's congregants no longer wear premodern or modern lenses. Rather, these three lenses exist simultaneously within them.

I cannot know exactly which lens a congregant uses to interpret a particular situation or event. What I do know, however, is that it is no longer an option for the church not to engage with postmodernism. Postmodernity is something that the church must apprehend to make Christianity relevant to people today through constructing alternative models for practices of care. It is time for the church to see the world through the lenses of its congregants. As I have dwelt on the question of where postmodern pastoral care and counseling for never-married single women needs to head, the two postmodern approaches of discourse theory and social constructionism have commended themselves as conversation partners that offer means for empowering never-married single women.

In light of discourse theory, the subjugated status of singleness becomes overtly evident in relation to the dominant discourse of marriage and family. Foucault's illumination of how power and knowledge work has enabled me to realize the intricately interwoven relationship between power and knowledge. The influence of social constructionism on the concept of therapy within a family therapy circle illumines the context within which I wish to reconstruct postmodern pastoral practices. In light of social constructionist ideas, I will briefly introduce socially constructed aspects of marriage and family, drawing on the works of Jon Berquist and Stephanie Coonzt, because it is critical for ministers and never-married single women to understand various forms of marriage and family in order to envision alternatives.

I will explain the shifts regarding the concept of therapy within the family therapy circle after first explicating the characteristics of discourse theory and social constructionism in relation to the issue of singleness. My purpose here is not to give a full exegesis of the extensive development of these two theories, but to show how concealed oppression has become treacherously entrenched in our daily lives, relegating never-married single women to the status of second-class citizens, and how never-married single women have internalized dominant cultural narratives as parts of their identities.

---

3. Graham, *Transforming Practice*, 3.

Discourse theory and social constructionism offer significant implications for the field of pastoral care and counseling because they enable serious critical social analysis for recognizing various subtle forms of oppression. In addition, these two approaches have compelled my attention because of their emphasis on voices from the margins. I think these two aspects can help the field empower the church to recover its core essence of embodying Jesus' radical hospitality toward all people.

According to Graham, "postmodernity, and the crisis of values it delineates and represents, is more than just a set of ideas. It concerns visions of ideal communities and human relationships in concrete terms."[4] I consider discourse theory and social constructionism great conversation partners for sharpening the field and improving the ministries of churches. In light of postmodern approaches, I will describe in Chapter 7 my detailed vision for a more inclusive church through pastoral practices responsive to the narratives of never-married single women.

5.2. The Issue of Oppression and Marginalization in Light of Pastoral Practices

One of my favorite verses from the Bible is from the Gospel of John. Jesus said, "I have come that they may have life, and have it more abundantly."[5] This verse has direct implications for the field of pastoral care and counseling to the extent that the ultimate concern of pastoral care is persons' well-being. Stephen Pattison finds a commonality between liberation theology and pastoral care in that the primary interests of both are "people's well-being and flourishing" and "the actual practice of increasing human flourishing."[6] Is today's church a place where never-married women experience abundant life here and now? How can the church be a catalyst for bringing about shalom for God's people? (I will answer these questions in Chapter 7.) How does the field of pastoral care and counseling enable ministers to continue what Jesus asked us to do: to help all people have life more abundantly?

I do not think that teaching never-married single women how to find and catch their Mr./Ms. Rights will miraculously bring abundant life to these women. Nor will spiritualizing the state of singleness. I do not want

---

4. Ibid., 13.
5. John 10:10.
6. Pattison, *Pastoral Care and Liberation Theology*, 4.

to devalue the teaching of skills for dating or the focus on spirituality that churches strategically utilize for never-married single populations. These techniques will enhance the quality of life of never-married single women to some extent. For me, however, the field of pastoral care and counseling needs to pay attention to subtle forms of oppression in order to empower never-married single women to experience abundant life.

Since the Peruvian Catholic priest Gustavo Gutiérrez offered the first formal outlines of liberation theology at a pastoral conference in Chimbote, Peru, in July 1968, the theme of liberation has challenged the theory and practice of pastoral care in many parts of the so-called Third World.[7] Latin America's liberation theology has become enormously influential within the theological enterprise, along with James Cone's Black liberation theology, through rigorous concern for the liberation of the oppressed and the poor from unjust systems. Upholding the necessity of the integration of personal and social healing in order to retrieve the prophetic heritage of the field, Howard Clinebell early on esteemed the value of liberation theology in terms of its implications for pastoral practices. Clinebell stated that "liberation theology should become a major conceptual resource in both our theory and practice."[8]

In fact, liberation theology has helped other pastoral theologians, including Larry Graham (1992) and Pattison (1994), realize the importance of socio-political analysis in order to liberate persons from oppressive structures. Pastoral practices from the perspective of the communal contextual paradigm resonate with the emphases of liberation theology. Specifically, suggesting the concept of "psychosystemic" as opposed to the term, "psychodynamic," on which the classical individualistic model of care heavily relied, Graham calls attention to the wider context of each troubled individual. He regards treating individuals in isolation from their larger cultural, ideological, or political contexts as being like throwing straw into the wind.[9] Authentic healing can be ensured when larger forces are dealt with alongside seeking changes in individuals.

Pattison endeavors to establish the relevance of liberation theology for the field of pastoral care and counseling in his book, *Pastoral Care and*

---

7. Lartey, *In Living Color: An Intercultural Approach to Pastoral Care and Counseling*, 113.

8. Clinebell, "Toward Envisioning the Future of Pastoral Counselingand AAPC," 189.

9. Graham, *Care of Persons, Care of Worlds*, 13.

Liberation Theology (1994). Liberation from spiritual and psychological bondage is not enough. Pattison's critique of individualistic pastoral care well exposes the limits of the clinical paradigm from a liberation theological perspective:

> Pastoral care has fallen into the trap of thinking too narrowly about how people's welfare might be sought and their potential developed. In so doing, it may actually inadvertently work against its intentions to promote well-being; it may also collude with some of the social and political forces which create and maintain human suffering.[10]

Insights from liberation theology have provided the field with a necessary awareness of a wider context through the critical lenses of socio-political analysis. Jim Poling (1991), Elain Graham (1996), and Lartey (2003) also actively build dialogues with liberation theology as they wrestle with suggesting pastoral practices. Interest in the issue of oppression has enlarged the concepts of pastoral practices to include relational justice that is involved in the redistribution of power, resources, and privilege.

I appreciate the book *Injustice and the Care of Souls* (2009) for taking the issue of oppression seriously in order to "broaden and inform the paradigm for pastoral care in a variety of contexts and communities, including the poor, the homeless, the abused, the aged, and racial/ethnic communities."[11] With the principal postulation that pastoral care is deeply related to justice and compassion, the twenty-two authors in this volume suggest their constructive views on pastoral care in terms of injustice and oppression. Although all human beings suffer one way or the other, some people's pains are more bearable than others' within our human systems.

These authors argue that skilled ministers need the ability to both recognize and analyze the impact of oppression on individuals and faith communities in order to fulfill their prophetic role of bringing healing, voice, and wholeness to the marginalized.[12] I think their assertion and Miller-McLemore's view illumine each other. According to Miller-McLemore, "When those involved in pastoral care do not know how to recognize the realities of violence toward women, they foster further damage and violence."[13] It is a must for the field to equip those who provide pastoral

---

10. Pattison, *Pastoral Care and Liberation Theology*, 208.
11. Kujawa-Holbrook and Montagno, "Introduction," 1.
12. Ibid., 2.
13. Miller-McLemore, "The Living Human Web," 20.

care and counseling with the knowledge to identify various forms of oppression, not only to reclaim the prophetic role but also to prevent further injustices.

In light of this line of thought, the issue of oppression is significant for never-married single women because the oppression under which these women exist is an unrecognized oppression. It is problematic that both ministers and never-married single women are unaware of the ways in which injustices are perpetrated in single women's lives. As I interacted with my ten research partners during our interviews and with the single women attending the day-long workshop I mentioned earlier, I realized the seriousness of invisible oppression. Without a framework, it is hard to discern. During the single women's workshop, I seemed to be the only person who felt offended by the main speaker's irrelevant (in my eyes) materials.

Unfortunately, never-married single women have rarely been recognized as those at the margins because oppression toward them is so embedded in our dominant culture that not many people are able to discern it. That is why I call it "subtle oppression," and we need a better tool to examine it. There is a parallel between this subtle oppression and "the Dream" that Ta-Nehisi Coates refers to in his book, *Between the World and Me* (2015). The Dream of American dominant culture is invisibly embedded in all of American society, and it feeds into the dangers black men face in this country. Coates faces the concrete reality that his son could be another Trayvon Martin. Recounting the pervasive culture of his childhood that denied black beauty by depicting "everyone of any import, from Jesus to George Washington,"[14] as white in movies, on television, or in textbooks, Coates urges people to interrogate the dominant culture and its ideologies ruthlessly. He asserts that "an unceasing interrogation of the stories told to us by the schools" is now felt to be essential in order to dismantle the violence that undergirds the country.[15]

Perhaps it is ruthless interrogation that will help us bring the subtle oppression under which never-married single women live into the light. In other words, I think such oppression can be identified only through critical examination because of its concealment within taken-for-granted reality. I demand that the field of pastoral care and counseling equip ministers to discern concealed oppression in today's world. The ability to discern disguised forms of oppression is a required skill for ministers who hope to

---

14. Coates, *Between the World and Me*, 43.
15. Ibid., 34.

bring about wholeness for never-married single women. To help ministers do so, I will introduce a better tool for analyzing the issue of singleness. Before I do that, allow me to share more about the oppressive situations that never-married women face.

5.3. Invisible Oppression

Some people might say that it is inappropriate to approach the issue of singleness from the perspective of marginalization or oppression. Some might accuse me of being alarmist or over-reactive, of making a big deal out of nothing. They might question my ability to intelligibly approach the issue of singleness in churches in the twenty-first century from this perspective because there seems to be no overt oppression of never-married single women. The oppression under which never-married single women suffer, however, is not about physical coercion or forceful duress. It is something invisible, but it surely exists. Foucault's notions of modern power and classical power ("sovereign power") especially in *Discipline and Punish: The Birth of the Prison* (1977) can shed light on this point.

Contrasting modern power with sovereign power, Foucault talks about a positive side of power. What he means by positive, however, is not something healthy or desirable. Instead, it is something that constitutes our lives. The meaning of the positive side of power gets clearer through Foucault's following remarks:

> We must cease once and for all to describe the effects of power in negative terms: it 'excludes', it 'represses', it 'censors', it 'abstracts', it 'masks', it 'conceals'. In fact, power produces; it produces reality; it produces domains of objects and rituals of truth. The individual and the knowledge that may be gained of him belong to this production.[16]

Classical power is something negative in that a feudal lord exerted his power to subjugate particularly with sword. In contrast, modern power is understood in a positive sense to the extent that it produces "truths" shaping our lives. That is, constructed ideas become norms to dictate people's ways of being. (I will elaborate more details below in light of the Panopticon and discourse theory.) It is important to remember that forms of oppression from modern power have become insidiously invisible.

---

16. Foucault, *Discipline and Punish*, 194.

According to constructive theologian Namsoon Kang, "We live in a world where the centre/the colonizer/the oppressor is often invisible and disguised."[17] Oppression has become so insidious that people experience it without knowing that they do. I have found it problematic that neither ministers nor never-married single women are aware of the injustice of the ways in which the marriage and family discourse forms their lives and their senses of self. That's why I am deeply moved by Carol Lakey Hess's view that considers implicit and unrecognized "girl-denying" tendencies more threatening to the futures of girls reared in mainline churches than flagrant misogyny.[18] People can be under surveillance and control without experiencing any physical coercion. Subtly invisible oppression can be more harmful than blatant oppression.

Donald Chinula makes it clear that oppression can exist in a seemingly peaceful context. Explicating four tasks of oppression-sensitive pastoral caregiving, Chinula names the phenomenon of "contained violence," which is sustained by the acquiescence of the oppressed in order to keep the peace.[19] If someone decides to tolerate an injustice in order to keep the peace, it is not peace but contained violence. Chinula asserts, "Such peace obscures and shields obscene oppression, exploitation, and dehumanization."[20] Although never-married women might not consciously choose to tolerate overt injustices done to them, I perceive the current external peace as contained violence because of the tyranny of the dominant marriage and family discourse that tacitly dictates people's ways of being.

The identity of the cloaked oppression under which never-married single women suffer is revealed through the concept of Panopticism. The Panopticon is an architectural form developed by Jeremy Bentham in the eighteenth century. It is a circular building divided into cells at the periphery surrounding the central courtyard. The outer walls of each cell are glass. A tower is at the center of the form with wide windows that allow supervisors to observe individuals in each cell. They are distinctly outlined against the window on the opposite side of the cell. I consider Panopticism, as described by Foucault in *Discipline and Punish*, a useful instrument for

---

17. Kang, "Theology from a Space Where Postcolonialism and Feminism Intersect," 61.

18. Hess, *Caretakers of Our Common House*, 14.

19. Chinula, "The Tasks of Oppression-Sensitive Pastoral Caregiving and Counseling," 135.

20. Ibid.

making invisible oppression visible. Foucault considers the Panopticon structure "a design of subtler coercion."[21]

The building's design allows supervisors in the tower to observe persons in the cells, and it prohibits the persons in the cells from seeing the supervisors. "In the peripheric ring, one is totally seen, without ever seeing; in the central tower, one sees everything without ever being seen."[22] In addition, the sidewalls of the cells forbid individuals from communicating with each other. Therefore, whereas individuals are the objects of information, they can never be subjects in communication with one another. The absence of communication robs them of an opportunity to compare their experiences. As a result, they can neither generate alternatives nor ally themselves against this subjugation. Those persons confined in the spaces cannot help but assume that they can be the subject of a supervisor's gaze at any time.

In Foucault's view, the Panopticon is the most effective way to make inmates into docile bodies that could be more easily used and manipulated because it produces "a state of conscious and permanent visibility that assures the automatic functioning of power."[23] The Panopticon leads inmates to experience themselves as the subjects of an ever-present gaze. The watchfulness of supervisors becomes so internalized within people that, in the end, their own internalized gaze automatically controls them. I understand Foucault's Panopticon as corresponding to the concept of sociocultural narratives.

I think the dominant discourse that considers never-married single women "spinsters," connoting unattractiveness or failure, has functioned as a Panopticon for never-married single women. One of my interviewees' remarks demonstrates how this works among people:

> When I first joined XXX Church, I saw many older single women, Unnideul, in leadership positions, Gansa. My friends and I all thought we might end up like them. So I have never wanted to become a Gansa [leader] because being a Gansa means the road to being a "*nocheonyu* (老處女)." So we didn't want that title at all because we associate Gansa with nocheonyu.

In a later interview, Kristine (a 31-year-old Ph.D. student) defined the Korean term *nocheonyu*: "I will translate it as an involuntarily unmarried

21. Foucault, *Discipline and Punish*, 209.
22. Ibid., 208.
23. Ibid., 201.

woman that has a very negative connotation, like 'unwanted woman.'" The dominant discourse about never-married single women caused not only Kristine but also a number of her friends to cease their active involvement in church at some point.

According to '"[24] This explains the experience of Kathy (a 34-year-old registered nurse) "feeling left behind" when most of her friends had gotten married. I suspect what Denham describes might be a factor in Kathy's feeling left behind and alone. Negative cultural biases against never-married single women blinded Kathy to seeing her professional success. Once never-married single women internalize the labels given them by the dominant discourse, external stimuli are no longer required to coerce them. In his classic work, *Identity, Youth, and Crisis*, Erik Erikson captures the sociocultural narrative regarding the value of women and marriage:

> For the student of development and the practitioner of psychoanalysis knows that the stage of life crucial for the emergence of an integrated female identity is the step from youth to maturity, the state when a young woman, whatever her work or career, relinquishes the care received from the parental family in order to commit herself to the love of a stranger and to the care to be given to his and her offspring.[25]

Erikson regarded marriage as the turning point that indicated the maturity of a woman. No matter how old a woman is, she remains immature if she has never married. Personally, I have experienced this through my involvement in local churches, both in South Korea and in the United States. Congregants easily extend more respect to married male colleagues, even if they are younger than I am. Only when a woman commits herself to the love of an unknown man and to taking care of their children is the integration of her female identity completed. Otherwise, never-married single women are selfish and abnormal. The negative sociocultural narratives about single women have been dominant not only in society in general but in churches as well. Although church needs to be a place where women can experience transformation of cultural narratives, churches have taught women to conform to those narratives.

Single women's self-narratives have not had an opportunity to flower into their own colors and shapes in response to the question of who we are able to be. Instead, we have been told who we should be by the sociocultural

---

24. Denham, "Life-Styles: A Culture in Transition," 167.
25. Erikson, *Identity, Youth, and Crisis*, 265.

narratives surrounding us. According to Jill Freedman and Gene Combs, sociocultural stories influence the ways people interpret their daily experiences, and people's daily actions influence the stories that circulate in society.[26] It is inevitable that sociocultural narratives are inextricably woven into persons' self-narratives. As members of the wider society, women cannot escape the clout of these sociocultural narratives. With this in mind, Bons-Storm's assertion that "women's self-narratives cannot be listened to without realizing that gender expectations and gender roles play an important part" makes more sense.[27]

Sociocultural narratives have power over individuals as they form a sense of self. In this vein, Emma Justes' admonition to ministers providing pastoral care to women is worth considering. Justes states, "Pastoral counseling with women requires that culturally defined stereotypes be questioned and challenged and that new images of women be allowed to blossom."[28] Justes' major concern is for women experiencing physical and sexual violence, yet her advice is also very relevant to never-married single women. One of the most important pastoral tasks is to empower never-married single women to break free from the pejorative cultural narratives that define their existence. In the meantime, however, it might be effective to empower never-married single women to simply change their relationship to those cultural narratives until their eradication becomes reality.

Abolishing a social constriction is not an easy task. Eradicating the internalized influence of predominant sociocultural narratives is even harder than relinquishing an apparent social restriction. Elizabeth Cady Stanton averred that "women's oppression cannot be overcome without liberation from restrictive and repressive social authority, including those forms of authority that are internalized."[29] I cannot agree more with Stanton that the mere elimination of ostensibly repressive social regulations cannot bring women's oppression to an end. Eradication of exploitive social conventions and inculcated restrictions within must happen simultaneously.

This is true not only for women's oppression but also for all kinds of oppression. Suzanne Lipsky talks about the detrimental effects internalized oppression has had on every existing black group. In Lipsky's view, it is internalized racism that has been "a major factor preventing us, as black

---

26. Freedman and Combs, *Narrative Therapy*, 17.
27. Bons-Storm, *The Incredible Woman*, 47.
28. Justes, "Women," 298.
29. Clark and Richardson, eds., *Women and Religion*, 249.

people, from realizing and putting into action the tremendous intelligence and power which in reality we possess."[30] Even after constricting social regulations are removed, if people are not released from their own internalization of those dominant discourses' teachings, people's subjugation will not come to an end. The marginalization of never-married single women becomes evident when I examine it through the lens of discourse theory.

5.4. Dominant Discourse vs. Subordinate Discourse

Discourse theory is "one of an array of postmodern approaches to knowledge that asks how meaning is constructed."[31] Beginning with Foucault and Lyotard, postmodernists prefer multiple methods of interpretation instead of universalizing truth claims. The word *discourse* has its root in the Latin *discurrere*, which is a combination of two words, *dis* and *currere*: *dis* means "away" and *currere* means "to run." Thus, its literal meaning is "running to and fro." *Discourses* denotes numerous discourses, big and small, running back and forth in any culture. I think Lyotard's term, *metanarratives*, is a concept that corresponds to "dominant discourse."

Rachel Hare-Mustin defines *discourse* as "a system of statements, practices, and institutional structures that share common values."[32] As various discourses circulate and compete with one another in a given society, they generate a set of verbal and nonverbal codes and conventions through which they enact their influences on people's behaviors and attitudes. This explicates the predicament that, while it is humans who produce discourses, we are often overpowered by them. Foucault states, "We are judged, condemned, classified, determined in our undertakings, destined to a certain mode of living or dying" by the truths we create.[33] Circulated sociocultural narratives are constructed by human beings, yet these narratives frequently dictate our ways of being.

Not all circulating discourses have the same influences: some have a central influence, while others are relegated to the margins. For example, whereas the marriage and family discourse is a domineering force in general, both in church and in society, people have not paid attention to the discourse of singleness. According to Hare-Mustin, "One way to assess the

30. Lipsky, "Internalized Oppression," 94.
31. Hare-Mustin, "Discourses in the Mirrored Room," 20.
32. Ibid., 19.
33. Foucault, *Power/Knowledge*, 94.

relative dominance or marginalization of a discourse is to ask what institutions and ways of being are supported by the discourse."[34] Given that the whole society, including churches, promote marriage and family, subordination of single people's discourse is foreseeable.

However, it is important to know that just because a discourse is dominant does not mean it is legitimate or grounded on scientific evidence or supremacy. Rather, "the dominant discourses both produce and are produced by social interaction, a particular language community, and the socioeconomic context."[35] (I will elaborate this process in more detail when I converse with social constructionism). To become a dominant discourse, a discourse must play a critical role in a time or place; who is speaking or writing and to or for whom they are speaking is crucial. Institutional and historical constraints also play roles in the formation of discourses and their power in society. In other words, who is in the position of power and what ideologies this certain group supports weigh more than their discourse's inherent truthfulness.

This is what Foucault's book, *Power/Knowledge*, is about. Its title points to the complexly intertwined relationships between power and knowledge. Foucault argues, "There is no point in dreaming of a time when knowledge will cease to depend on power. . . . It is not possible for power to be exercised without knowledge, it is impossible for knowledge not to engender power."[36] Power and knowledge interplay, bilaterally exchanging influences. Whatever those in power promote can be perceived as truth. This intertwined relationship between power and knowledge leads me to worry about the recent history textbook controversy in South Korea.

The Diplomat, an online international news magazine, reports, "A South Korea court ruled in favor of allowing the Ministry of Education to mandate history textbook revisions."[37] Actually, it is the president, Geun-hye Park, who holds the position to rewrite high school history textbooks, with support from her right-wing government officials. In light of Foucault's wisdom regarding the relationship between power and knowledge, I am concerned about the possibility of knowledge (history) being distorted by

---

34. Hare-Mustin, "Discourses in the Mirrored Room," 21.
35. Ibid., 20.
36. Foucault, *Power/Knowledge*, 52.
37. Denney, "South Korea's History Textbook Controversy," *The Diplomat*, April 4, 2015, https://web.archive.org/web/*/http://thediplomat.com/2015/04/south-koreas-history-textbook-controversy/.

the powerful through the omission and highlighting of particular aspects of historical events. Although it lies beyond the limits of this study to review all of modern Korean history, I will point out a few pivotal historical facts to explain my discomfort with this history textbook controversy.

According to Wikipedia, Chung-hee Park, the father of the current president, was the "*de facto* leader of the country since leading [the] Coup d'état of May Sixteenth in 1961, which effectively overthrew the Second Republic of Korea."[38] Given there are people who glamorize this military Coup d'état as a revolution, it is a red flag for me. Chung-hee Park was the president of South Korea from 1962 to 1978. He was assassinated by Jae-Kyu Kim, the director of Korean Central Intelligence Agency, in order to prevent the mass killings in the provinces of Busan and Masan that Chung-hee Park and his governmental officials were about to perpetrate. I do not want to gainsay the extraordinary economic development that took place in South Korea during Chung-hee Park's regime. Nevertheless, injustices must not be justified or glamorized in any way. Thus, I think governmental officials should be forbidden from writing histories, since this can become a means to sustaining their own power and privilege longer.

Juxtaposing dominant discourses with subordinate discourses, Hare-Mustin points out that "discourses associated with groups on the margins of society are excluded from influence. They are not spoken with authority. They arouse discomfort."[39] When a person from the margins questions dominant discourses, people raise their eyebrows and feel discomfort because dominant discourses are what they take for granted. Dominant discourses are so embedded in our day-to-day practices that it is hard to question them. In fact, much of our recurring cultural practices are formed around dominant discourses, from simple greetings to marriages and funerals.

Therefore, it can be concluded that "dominant discourses support and reflect the prevailing ideologies in the society."[40] Cultural practices in a society reflect the discourses the society values or despises. Thus, discourses contribute to maintaining a certain worldview, bringing "certain

---

38. Wikipedia, s.v. "List of Presidents of South Korea," last modified March 27, 2016, https://web.archive.org/web/*/https://en.wikipedia.org/wiki/List_of_Presidents_of_South_Korea

39. Hare-Mustin, "Discourses in the Mirrored Room," 21.

40. Ibid., 19.

phenomena into sight and obscur[ing] other phenomena."⁴¹ Whereas what corresponds to dominant discourses is supported, subordinate discourses are barely noticed. Hare-Mustin introduces a classic example of this:

> The Reagan era of the 1980s promoted a conservative, pro-family ideology that saw women defined by their crucial role in the family, and this at a time when competing discourses centered on women's independence and choice. The dominant discourse of masculine and feminine differences views women as essentially caring, close to nature, and oriented to meeting the needs of others, whereas men are essentially independent and achieving. Considerable effort in the biological and social sciences goes into supporting this prevailing view and trying to identify miniscule differences between men and women. Empirical research that finds differences gets published in scientific journals and touted in the popular media; empirical research that finds no differences rarely gets published in scientific journals or even mentioned in the popular media.⁴²

Femininity and masculinity are not essential components of who women and men truly are. Rather, these concepts are socially constructed to support social, political, religious, and patriarchal purposes. Dominant discourses are socially constructed, and so are sociocultural narratives. Although sociocultural narratives are socially constructed to privilege a certain group of people and degrade others, people are prone to believe them as if they are true. Negative stereotyping of never-married single women is not truth but a byproduct of a social process. Hence, single women must not assume these stereotypes as parts of their self-narratives.

Reasons for generally circulated cultural practices or ideas do not lie inherently in themselves. Rather, they can be found in their relationships with the dominant discourse. Pattison's report on the unpopularity of liberation theology under right-wing governments in British and North American societies between the late 1970s and the early 1980s can be understood in light of this line of thought. Pattison states, "For the most part liberation theology has not flowered amongst Christians in the Northern hemisphere."⁴³ Liberation theology was not widely accepted because the theory and practices that liberation theology promotes did not correspond

---

41. Ibid., 20.
42. Ibid., 22.
43. Pattison, *Pastoral Care and Liberation Theology*, 3.

to the dominant discourse of capitalism that right-wing governments endorsed.

When I think about the relationship between power and the dominant discourse, I can put into perspective the nagging question regarding the lack of literature that arose for me as I worked on my literature review. I suspect that the paucity of literature regarding never-married single women can be explained through the lens of discourse theory. Luther Baker's empirical research, "The Personal and Social Adjustment of the Never-Married Woman," published in 1968, and Margaret Adams' book, *Single Blessedness*, published in 1976, did not gain social attention, in spite of their truthfulness, because their assertions were not congruent with the dominant discourse about single women. The phenomena that the marriage and family discourse has always taken an absolute advantage over the discourse of singleness does not prove the inferiority of the single status nor the superiority of the married status. Instead, I think that the long period of the marginalized status of the discourse of singleness shows how few never-married people, never-married women in particular, have been in a position of power to write, speak, and eventually be heard on this topic.

In light of discourse theory's insights regarding the interplay of power and knowledge, James Clifford's understandings of ethnographic truths are apropos. Clifford considers ethnographic truths "inherently partial—committed and incomplete" because of ethnographers' inevitable partiality in their observations.[44] As the dictum, the "personal is political," indicates, no ethnographer is neutral. This underlying assumption of the authors in the book, *Writing Culture*, shatters any beliefs that one can clearly represent a culture. Like its subtitle, *The Poetics and Politics of Ethnography*, indicates, all the authors in this book, including Clifford, presuppose that the art of ethnography cannot be divorced from politics. For this reason, culture is understood not as an object to describe but as something "contested, temporal, and emergent."[45] As it emerges, its representation can only imply its reality.

What has been understood as a representation of a culture is deeply related to political power games. With this understanding in mind, I agree with Clifford's assertion that "all constructed truths are made possible by powerful 'lies' of exclusion and rhetoric." We need to remember that there have been countless subcultures that have been silenced and hidden under

---

44. Clifford, "Introduction: Partial Truth," 7.
45. Ibid., 19.

a few predominant cultural representations. The marriage and family discourse appears to show the way the world has been. Yet, its truth claims can be maintained only through the assent of the majority, who agree to silence or simply ignore voices from single persons. Understanding social constructionism will make this socially constructed reality more palpable.

5.5. Social Constructionism

Along with discourse theory, I find particular relevance for my current study in social constructionist ideas. Social constructionist ideas are vital to understanding the issue of singleness in a broader context. The approach called "social constructionism" has evolved and bloomed only within recent decades. With over 25 years of involvement with the development of constructionist ideas, Gergen considers the term *postmodernism* a very general term and social constructionism a specific outcome of postmodernism.[46] Hence, social constructionism may be understood as one of the branches of the tree called "postmodernism."

Although there is no single book or school of philosophy that represents all scholars' definitions of social constructionism, I will outline a few major foundational understandings of social constructionism in light of Gergen's book, *An Invitation to Social Construction*. In Gergen's view, there are three intellectual movements that stir contemporary dialogues in social construction: "the first illuminating the values inherent in all constructions of reality, the second the fragility of rational argument, and finally, the social basis of scientific knowledge."[47] In fact, these three contributors overlap what has brought postmodern epistemology out of modernity, as articulated in Chapter 1.

Hence, social constructionist ideas share the same epistemological bases as postmodernism in terms of rejecting the notion of objectively universal truth and challenging the supremacy of human reason and the very foundations of scientific knowledge. Social constructionism has brought a different understanding to the notion of knowledge. Whereas conventional knowledge was considered a map of the contours of the world, "social constructionism views discourse about the world not as a reflection or map

---

46. Gergen, *An Invitation to Social Construction*, 13–14.
47. Ibid., 26.

of the world but as an artifact of communal interchange."[48] It is people's agreement that confers power to knowledge.

From the perspective of social constructionism, reality is more what people construct together than something waiting to be found. People's concurrence makes something real. The most important aspect of social constructionism is the processes by which people come to agree with one another upon the world in which they live. Lynn Hoffman insightfully sums this up, saying, "social construction theory sees the development of knowledge as a social phenomenon and holds that perception can only evolve within a cradle of communication."[49] Nothing exists unless a circle of people agrees that it does. Extending this line of thinking, what makes something "normal" or "abnormal" does not intrinsically lie within it. Instead, the criteria for "normality" are greatly determined by people's assent to a set of ideas about what is "normal."

Challenging the objective basis of conventional knowledge, therefore, social constructionism invites people to be suspicious about the taken-for-granted world. Reasons for any prevailing form of understanding the world, no matter how many years it has been sustained, lie on the vicissitudes of social processes, such as communication, negotiation, conflict, and rhetoric, rather than on the empirical validity of the perspective in question.[50] Only when people within a community place the taken-for-granted behavior or belief into question does change become a possibility. In fact, human history consists of countless constructions and deconstructions of views brought about through incessant challenges.

As I was realizing how reality is constructed, I read an article in *Time* magazine about Jeralean Talley of Michigan, at 115 years old the oldest living person on April 8, 2015, according to the Gerontology Research Group. The article stated, "There could still be people who are older than Talley, but their claims have not been verified by the organization, which usually requires documentation such as original proof of birth, name change and recent identification."[51] What fascinated me was my reading between the lines of the article. That is, it was interesting to think about the numerous changes that Talley would have witnessed throughout her lifetime.

---

48. Gergen, "The Social Constructionist Movement in Modern Psychology," 266.
49. Hoffman, "Constructing Realities," 2.
50. Gergen, "The Social Constructionist Movement in Modern Psychology," 268.
51. Waxman, "Meet the World's New Oldest Living Person."

I wondered what she would consider the "normal" way(s) of the world, since she had experienced drastic changes over the course of her lifetime. Perhaps, she might not consider anything "normal" because of the unceasing challenges of norms once taken for granted. As an African American woman descended from African people enslaved in North Carolina, Karen B. Montagno, a pastoral theologian, has reminisced about the 1960s and 1970s as "a time of throwing off old racial norms and labels and claiming a self-defined identity."[52] As an African American female, Talley, I imagine, can relate to Montagno's remarks.

I wonder what it was like for Talley to go through changes resulting from the Women's Rights Movement as well as the African American Civil Rights Movement. What did she think as she exercised suffrage as a reality that was not possible for her mother or her grandmother even to imagine? Not only changes in the status of African Americans and women but also a lot of changes that have affected various aspects of people's ways of life have taken place during the past 115 years in the United States. One can assume that Talley's reality would have been tentative and ever-changing throughout her lifetime.

The reality that taught Talley to consider herself less than White people and men has been altered. At one time it was not acceptable for Black people to dine with White people in a restaurant. Yet, it is no longer okay to treat people differently because of their skin color. As long as people agree that it is wrong to discriminate against human beings based on their skin color, it is no longer "normal" to designate certain seats for Blacks and others for Whites on the same bus. As I reflect on these changes, the meaning of Gergen's words becomes more comprehensible. Gergen writes, "Regardless of the stability or repetition of conduct, perspectives may be abandoned as their intelligibility is questioned within the community of interlocutors."[53] People cannot defend perspectives or views based on how long human beings have sustained them and their resulting practices.

The rules for negotiated agreement within communities are ambiguous and continuously evolving depending on the preferences of the people within communities. Enumerating a few social constructionist investigations into gender, emotion, suicide, belief, schizophrenia, altruism, and psychological disorders, Gergen indicates that each study verifies that "the objective criteria for identifying such 'behaviors,' 'events,' or 'entities'

---

52. Montagno, "Midwives and Holy Subversives," 4.
53. Gergen, "The Social Constructionist Movement in Modern Psychology," 268.

are shown to be either highly circumscribed by culture, history, or social context or altogether nonexistent."[54] The rules for social conventions are not static but inherently arbitrary and dynamic. In light of these social constructionist ideas, I want to examine the taken-for-granted realities in relation to marriage and family.

5.6. Social Construction of the Concept of Marriage and Family

Marriage and family appear to be realities that have been sustained as long as human beings have existed on the earth. This is just the way it is. After being born, human beings grow, get married, have their own offspring, and die. At least, this is what I thought before I critically engaged with my way of being as a never-married single woman in my early thirties. Like many girls who dream of living "happily ever after" with their own prince, I had this dream and assumed marriage and forming a family was everyone's destiny. I had never imagined that I would be single at this point in my life. But here I am talking about the socially constructed reality of marriage as a single woman.

To examine this social construction, it is necessary to look into the history of marriage and the family. Yet I can only touch on some highlights of this history in the space of this work. As Sylvia Yanagisako asserts, it is impossible to "construct a precise, reduced definition for what are inherently complex, multifunctional institutions imbued with a diverse array of cultural principles and meanings."[55] Nevertheless, I want ministers and never-married single women to have an opportunity to view marriage and family as a socially constructed reality because it will provide them with some clues to imagining alternatives.

According to Coontz, "Only when we have a realistic idea of how families have and have not worked in the past can we make informed decisions about how to support families in the present or improve their future prospects."[56] I do not think her words are true only for helping ministers support diverse families. Understanding the various ways of families will enable ministers to provide proper care for never-married single women.

---

54. Ibid., 267.

55. Yanagisako, "Family and Household," 200, quoted in Coontz, *The Social Origins of Private Life*, 11.

56. Coontz, *The Way We Never Were*, 5–6.

Specifically, recognizing the socially constructed nature of marriage and families can offer both ministers and never-married single women the power to resist sociocultural narratives that dictates their ways of being.

For example, it was an eye-opening experience for me to read Coontz's research on the history of marriage and family in the United States as presented in the following volumes: *The Social Origins of Private Life* (1988), which provides a historical and analytical history of American families between 1600 and 1900; *The Way We Never Were* (1992), which gives a conventional chronological account of American family life from 1900 to 1990 as a sequel to the previous book; and Coontz's more recent work, *Marriage, a History* (2005). Perhaps it is my lens of social constructionism that makes Coontz's approaches to marriage and family more remarkable for me. In the midst of reading her texts, I murmured to myself, "Why didn't anyone teach me this before?" If I had known about these dimensions of marriage and family, my response to my singleness would have been different.

As a very goal-oriented person, I put getting married on my New Year's resolution list when I turned thirty, not because I wanted to get married or had a boyfriend but because my father's worry seemed to grow bigger having his baby daughter alone in a foreign land. I also felt social pressure that made me think that if I wanted to ever get married, it was better to do so sooner than later. I prayed about it and made efforts to form relationships. After three years passed by, I was still single and unhappy. As I reflected on my unhappiness with my life, I realized that I was not happy because I was not able to accomplish a goal that was ultimately out of my control. Then I realized how absurd it was to put "get married" on my New Year's resolution list for three consecutive years.

When I turned 33, I eliminated marriage from my New Year's resolutions and tried not to think about it. My energy level was boosted as I focused on what I really wanted to do with my life. When I look back, I feel grateful for my decision. Not having any tool to frame my singleness, I still happened to choose the best course for me. If I had understood the socially constructed characteristics of marriage, the first three years of my thirties would have been different. I hope ministers and never-married single women can learn that what we think is normal is a very contextual product.

Simply think about the presentations of marriage and family in the Hebrew Bible. In particular, let us consider Jacob's family. Jacob's love story with Rachel did not unfold as today's reader might expect it to. To make a long story short, Jacob ended up with two wives, Leah and Rachel, and two concubines, Bilhad and Zilpah, and had twelve children from these four women.[57] What really happened in his family is beyond our imagination. I do not think that even an author for an MTV sitcom could come up with such a story. What was "normal" in Jacob's time is totally "abnormal" and could be interpreted as "dysfunctional" in our time. Specifically, what strikes me is the verse that says, "Jacob was in love with Rachel and said, 'I'll work for you seven years in turn for your younger daughter Rachel.'"[58] I am struck because the verse sounds so similar to my own worldview. Jacob's whole story seems to reflect the realities of a distant past, except for his love for Rachel. However, did ancient people really get married because of love?

Given that the condition of romantic love for marriage is a pretty recent concept, Jacob's reason for choosing his spouse is astonishing. People have certainly fallen in love for thousands years. However, until recently, "marriage was not fundamentally about love. It was too vital an economic and political institution to be entered into solely on the basis of something as irrational as love."[59] Political and economic reasons have overridden romantic love as people have arranged marriages for centuries. Along the way, people have sometimes fallen in love, even with their spouses. As I consider Jacob's unusual reasons for wanting to marry Rachel, I wonder whether ancient Hebrew people's marriage customs were different from ones in Europe and the United States, the regions of Coontz's research focus.

In his book, *Controlling Corporeality: The Body and the Household in Ancient Israel* (2002), Jon Berquist sheds lights on my question. He shows that the social institution of marriage in ancient Israel was not the same as marriage in the modern Western world. Although the concept of the sexually bonded pair has been considered the fundamental building block of Israel, Berquist perceives that the matter of Israelite marriage is not as clear as often thought. He supports this reasoning with the following argument:

> The common scholarly portrayals of Israelite marriages and Israelite families that are assumed to be the primary contexts for sexuality and sexual expression are often based upon modern (and often romanticized) assumptions about what the family must be, rather than an observation of the ancient Israelite situation itself.[60]

---

57. Genesis 29 and 30.
58. Genesis 29:18.
59. Coontz, *Marriage, a History*, 7.
60. Berquist, *Controlling Corporeality*, 60.

In order to prove his assertion that "the modern construction of sexuality in terms of wives and husbands, therefore, does not pertain to the ancient world of Israel," Berquist points out the problem of interpreting the Hebrew Bible in English.[61] The Hebrew Bible is missing such words as *wife, wives, husband, husbands,* and even *marriage*.

Translators have translated the Hebrew words for *woman/women* to *wife/wives* and *man/men* to *husband/husbands* whenever "there is a clear reference to marriages."[62] Therefore, the reason why people today perceive similar ideas of marriage and family to their own in the Hebrew Bible is because modern translators have imposed their values on the texts as they have translated them. I have no doubt that the concept of marriage and family in ancient Israelite society was quite different from contemporary Western ideas about it. For example, Berquist notes, "A good head of household would father children with several women in the house, creating a household of increasing numbers and growing strength."[63] In other words, polygamous relationships were the norm.

In contrast, Coontz calls our attention to the concept of the ideal U.S. family from the 1950s. In fact, 1950s marriages were unique in many ways. Until that decade, relying on a single breadwinner had been rare. For thousands of years, most women and children had shared the tasks of making a living with men.[64] When it comes to the idea of a "traditional family," some might think about an extended family with two or three generations together. Yet, many people, including myself, would think of a family as only consisting of a working father, a full-time homemaker mother who wears an apron and waits on her husband and children, and dependent children.

Referring to this as the "Ozzie and Harriet" or "Leave it to Beaver" model, Coontz maintains that fewer than ten percent of American families meet this 1950s sit-com model.[65] Like the title of her book indicates, it is indeed "the way we never were." Since it describes something unrealistic and even impossible, Coontz calls this 1950s family model "a myth." Although she values myths in terms of bringing people together and promoting social solidarity, Coontz argues that the "recurring search for a traditional family model denies the diversity of family life, both past and present, and leads

---

61. Ibid., 62.
62. Ibid., 60.
63. Ibid., 65.
64. Coontz, *Marriage, a History*, 4.
65. Coontz, *The Way We Never Were*, 23.

to false generalizations about the past as well as wildly exaggerated claims about the present and the future."[66] I think her assertion has very significant implications for churches' pastoral practices today.

Specifically, I want to encourage Korean churches that designate the month of May "family month" to dwell on her remarks. As long as this unrealistic "traditional" family gets promoted from the pulpit, solidarity will be eroded and the confidence of people whose families "fall short" will be weakened. Considering the unprecedented rates of divorce, single parenthood, and never-married singlehood, Korean churches must recognize whom they exclude by being obsessed with celebrating a "traditional family" to which congregants rarely can relate.

5.7. Social Constructivist Influence on the Concept of Therapy

Social constructionist ideas have influenced the field of family therapy in terms of reconstructing the definition of therapy. Drawing on Lynn Hoffman, Jill Freedman, and Gene Combs, I will explain how social constructionist ideas have contributed to the reconstruction of this definition. These three scholars' experiences of shifts in their own lenses for understanding therapy shed light on my struggle to envision a postmodern model of care and practices for never-married women in the postmodern world, thus enabling me to understand pastoral practices through the metaphor of narratives along with such pastoral theologians as Andrew Lester (1995), Christie Neuger (2001), Karen Scheib (2004), John Blevins (2005), Duane Bidwell (2013), and Suzanne Coyle (2013, 2014). I will engage with these pastoral theologians' works later in this chapter as well as in Chapter 6.

The shift from first-order cybernetics to second-order cybernetics within family therapy and the further engagement with social constructionist ideas to envision therapy through the metaphor of narrative has crystallized the postmodern turn in pastoral practices of care and counseling. Let me expound why. The word *cybernetics* was coined by Norbert Wiener in 1950. He derived the word "from a Greek root (*kubernetes*), which signifies the pilot of a boat,"[67] and described it as "the science of communication and control."[68] This metaphor filtered into the field of family therapy through

66. Ibid., 14.
67. Freedman and Combs, *Narrative Therapy*, 3.
68. Hoffman, "Constructing Realities," 1.

Gregory Bateson, "a British anthropologist who in the 1960s, was studying the family relations of schizophrenia at the Palo Alto Veterans Hospital in California."[69] Influenced by this metaphor, Bateson developed a theory of family therapy, "first-order cybernetics," which understands family as "systems."

In this theory, a family is compared to an organism or a machine. That is, just like there is a fixated cycle of routine activity in machines, human affairs entail the activity of a feedback cycle. Under the first-order cybernetics paradigm, the therapist is regarded as "a sort of repairman—a social engineer."[70] The main role of a therapist is to fix problems. When families are stuck in repetitive patterns of unsatisfying behaviors, a therapist needs to disrupt this dysfunctional cycle in order to redirect the family to healthier behaviors. When therapists actively design means of intervention under the clear understanding of what a functional family structure should be, families are supposed to receive the strategies that therapists design to address their pathologically recurring cycles of behaviors.

Regarding therapists' active stance, Christian Beels considers this model of family therapy "ultimately moralistic and prescriptive," stating that "the therapist was trying to get the family to improve according to a theory of healthy/unhealthy functioning that he or she understood better than did the family."[71] The metaphors of first-order cybernetics are rooted in a very modern way of thinking in that this theory assumes an objectively knowable truth, the ideal family, and a neutral observer, the therapist. In this paradigm, the therapist knows the way an ideal "family" is supposed to be. Since therapists are supposed to have authority to access this truth, there is a hierarchy between therapists, the experts, and clients, the sick. The "systems" metaphor has served the field well for many years.

Hoffman introduces her journey as a therapist with her encounter with the lens of first-order cybernetics in 1963. This encounter led her to depart from the concept of regarding a symptom as a property of the individual. It seems to me that Hoffman welcomed first-order cybernetics because it enabled her to analyze people's problems in a wider context, the family "system," which complemented her old paradigm based on the Freudian "archeological" metaphor which taught therapists to solve people's problems through delving into the depths of their unconscious minds. The

---

69. Beels, *A Different Story*, 87.

70. Hoffman, "A Constructivist Position for Family Therapy," 111.

71. Beels, *A Different Story*, 107.

lens of first-order cybernetics worked fine for about twenty years, until she ran into the philosophical position called "constructivism," which emerged to the surface in the 1980s.

"Constructivism holds that the structure of our nervous systems dictates that we can never know what is 'really' out there."[72] Heinz von Foerster's research on neural nets and experiments on the color vision of frogs by Humberto Maturana and his colleague verify that our brains do not function like cameras, reflecting images of the world as it is. Rather, images of the world are transmuted by human brains. Hoffman wrote her book, *Foundations of Family Therapy*, in 1980, through the lens of first-order cybernetics. By the time the book was going to be published, she had started becoming fonder of constructivists' critiques of the first-order cybernetics' stance toward therapy.

Therefore, "in an effort at self-correction," she states, "I wrote a prologue and an epilogue that attempted to point the way to a less control-oriented model, a model that did not place the therapist outside of, or above, the family."[73] A family therapist cannot keep a neutral stance as an objective observer and know the objective truth about others and the world. Instead, for Hoffman, a therapist had to consider therapy "an immersion into a larger system that included oneself and other professionals as well."[74] As a therapist interacts with a family, s/he becomes one of its members, not an outsider. This new approach to understanding therapy came to be known as "second-order cybernetics."

According to second-order cybernetics, "living systems were seen not as objects that could be programmed from the outside, but as self-creating, independent entities. They might be machines, but they were. . . . nontrivial machines, meaning that they were not determined by history nor did they follow any predictable path."[75] Being affected by a constructivist position, second-order cybernetics undermined the assumption that "therapy was a matter of instruction or manipulation of one person by another, who was by definition some kind of expert on how the other person ought to be."[76] Freedman and Combs also critique the metaphor of "guidance" to the extent that it gives too much credit to therapists for the changes that oc-

72. Hoffman, "A Constructivist Position for Family Therapy," 110.
73. Ibid., 112.
74. Ibid., 114.
75. Hoffman, "Constructing Realities," 5.
76. Ibid., 2.

cur.⁷⁷ Although it is clients that bring about changes in themselves and their lives, under this model, clients "experience themselves as passive recipients of external wisdom" along the way.⁷⁸ As a result, therapy fails to augment a sense of agency within clients.

Shortcomings of the metaphors of "system" and "structure" brought Freedman and Combs to eventually adopt the metaphor of "narrative" and the theory of social constructionism as ways to organize their clinical work. These models intrigue me. When therapists think of therapy in terms of the metaphor of structure, it obscures the constantly changing and evolving aspects of family relationships. Therapists are likely to fail to observe dynamically changing dimensions of families, not because this dimension is absent, but because the metaphor of structure becomes a defining lens through which therapists perceive families. The influence of this mode of seeing prevents therapists from noticing one of the essential characteristics of a family, that it is a living organism.

Freedman and Combs write, "It [the metaphor of structure] can freeze our perceptions in time and oversimplify complex interactions. It can invite us to treat people as objects, thus dehumanizing the therapeutic process."⁷⁹ Freedman and Combs have become more attracted to metaphors such as "stories" and "re-authoring," which are different from the first-order cybernetics' metaphors of system and structure. Their views on metaphors are well described in their book, *Symbol, Story, and Ceremony: Using Metaphor in Individual and Family Therapy* (1990). In fact, the shift from first-order cybernetics to second-order cybernetics can be understood as a metaphorical alteration. (I will discuss reasons for it in chapter 6.) Second-order cybernetics has re-visioned therapy in light of fresh metaphors, such as "ecosystemic epistemology," "coevolution," and "cocreation."⁸⁰

Of course, there were other influential factors, such as the Milan Systemic Family Therapy team and Milton Erickson, on Freedman and Combs' journey. Yet, they developed their idea of therapy around the metaphor of narratives after encountering Michael White, who introduced them to a postmodern worldview, including social constructionism. According to Alan Parry and Robert Doan, "White's influence on the field has

---

77. Freedman and Combs, *Narrative Therapy*, 4.
78. Ibid.
79. Ibid., 2.
80. Ibid., 5.

finally brought family therapy into the postmodern world."[81] Hoffman also thinks of therapy in relation to the metaphor of narratives because of the influence of social construction theory. Although Hoffman, Freedman, and Combs have embraced the second-order cybernetics' way of thinking in relation to therapy, they go further in developing their lenses by adopting social constructionist ideas that guide them to imagine therapy through the metaphor of narratives.

In spite of the commonality of rejecting an objectively knowable truth, constructivism is somewhat different from social constructionism in that each approach stresses different points. Whereas the former emphasizes the operations of the nervous system, the latter places far more emphasis on social interpretation and the intersubjective influences of language, family, and culture.[82] Describing the shift from constructivism to social constructionism, Gergen says that it is "from an experiential to a social epistemology."[83] In other words, constructionism focuses on how an individual constructs reality based on his/her personal experiences. Contrary to this, social constructionism is more interested in mutually constructed realities through interactions among people.

As I explicated previously, social constructionism presupposes that everything that makes up our social realities is socially constructed by members of a particular culture. An evolving set of meanings emerges from interactions among people. When therapy is understood through the metaphor of narratives and social constructionism, therapists no longer try to solve problems. When therapists began thinking of people's problems as stories that people agree to tell themselves, what they found they needed to do was to "bring forth and 'thicken' (Geertz, 1978) stories that did not support or sustain problems."[84] Thus, therapists' main job is to enable those who bring problem-saturated stories to discover alternative stories.

I think that understanding therapy in light of the metaphor of narratives and social constructionist ideas has important implications for pastoral practices for never-married single women in that they provide those performing a pastoral helping role with a theoretical foundation for creating subversive pastoral practices that enable single women to narrate their own unique stories with great freedom to imagine multiple ways to be.

81. Parry and Doan, *Story Re-Visions*, 17.
82. Hoffman, "Constructing Realities," 2.
83. Gergen, "The Social Constructionist Movement in Modern Psychology," 268.
84. Freedman and Combs, *Narrative Therapy*, 16.

There has, in fact, been a turn toward embracing constructivist/social constructivist perspectives and the metaphor of narratives within the field of pastoral care and counseling through the pastoral theologians I referenced previously. These pastoral theologians are consonant with one another in that they propose narrative practices as a model of pastoral care and counseling. They believe people's stories play a central role in their senses of self, providing them with meanings. This is true despite their varying target populations—women for Neuger, elderly women over 65 for Scheib, couples for Bidwell—and the different types of stories focused on—future stories for Lester and Scheib and shared stories for Bidwell. Although Lester is more grounded in a constructivist philosophy, all the others embrace the implicit assumptions of narrative theory regarding socially constructed meanings and interpretations of people's lives.

I think the following remarks from Stephen Madigan, which Bidwell also cites, recapitulate characteristics of narratives that Lester, Neuger, Scheib, and Coyle resonate with:

> The complexity of life, and how lives are lived, is mediated through the expression of the stories we tell. Stories are shaped by the surrounding dominant cultural context; some stories emerge as the long-standing reputations we live through, and often (often more preferred) stories of who we are (and might possibly become) can sometimes be restrained and pushed back to the margins of our remembered experiences. . . . But whatever the stories are that we tell (and don't tell), they are performed, live through us, and have abilities to both restrain and liberate our lives.[85]

Stories are critical for human beings. Indeed, human beings are multi-storied. Our senses of self and identity are built piece by piece as we pick and choose particular experiences, place them "into our stories and then integrate these stories into our ongoing core narratives" alongside numerous other stories.[86] Our stories are not fixed. Rather, they are flexible and changeable. In fact, it is the multifaceted and fluid aspects of our stories around which narrative pastoral theologians structure their practices of care.

Pointing to postmodern/poststructuralist philosophies as the basis for the narrative therapy approach, Neuger asserts, "Our interpretation of reality and the meanings we make out of it are socially constructed, . . .

---

85. Madigan, *Narrative Therapy*, 29–30.
86. Lester, *Hope in Pastoral Care and Counseling*, 30.

Therefore, we have the capacity to shift meanings and thus change the options available to us in dealing with life circumstances."[87] Hence, pastoral practices need to focus on empowering people to generate new language and lenses to articulate and see alternatives that will result in new possible realities. Our core stories often keep us from seeing alternatives and obscure other possible stories.

Grounded in a constructivist philosophy, Lester, in his book, *Hope in Pastoral Care and Counseling* (1995), puts an emphasis on the importance of the future dimension of time-consciousness in human existence in order to instill a sense of hope through theory building and pastoral practices. Critiquing pastoral practices rooted in personality theories and psychotherapeutic practices that overlook future orientation, Lester upholds that "pastoral care and counseling, to maintain integrity, must be rooted in a theological anthropology that includes awareness that a person's core narratives include stories from all three dimensions of human temporality: past, present, and future."[88] Specifically, people's future stories are the most significant elements to which pastoral caregivers must attend.

Correlating social constructionism and narrative theory for pastoral practices for elderly women over the age of 65, Scheib echoes Lester, stating, "Assisting in the creation of a hopeful future story is an important dimension of the narrative practice of care with older women."[89] In this light, Scheib considers pastoral care as narrative practice a helpful tool for finding alternative stories and challenging the stories that keep people in self-defeating interpretations. Along with Lester and Scheib, Neuger, Bidwell, and Coyle have stressed the narrative approach's potential to empower people to find alternative stories.

Given that postmodernity is somewhat unfamiliar terrain for the field of pastoral care and counseling, which is a byproduct of modernity, I appreciate these pastoral theologians' pioneering efforts to create new trails for imagining pastoral practices in relation to the metaphor of narratives and social constructionism. Their footsteps have invited the field of pastoral care and counseling to understand practices of care in light of the richness and challenges of postmodern epistemological sensitivity. Like a new road can be created by the steps of many people, I hope to join their footsteps in

---

87. Neuger, *Counseling Women*, 86.
88. Lester, *Hope in Pastoral Care and Counseling*, 41.
89. Scheib, *Challenging Invisibility*, 62.

order to broaden the trail and invite more people to see its potential to offer life-giving practices.

As I join their efforts, I will strengthen the liberative and egalitarian aspects of narrative practices they and other pastoral theologians have stressed. In addition, I want to enrich narrative practices, which are still dominantly studied by European Americans, by adding my Korean feminist view developed through engagement with the lived experiences of never-married Korean single women. Furthermore, I want to augment narrative practices by offering a vision for churches from a narrative perspective. Although Scheib calls the church to be "not only an inclusive community but a redemptive and prophetic community that opposes the marginalization of older women," most narrative approaches within the field seem to be satisfied with bringing changes only on an individualistic level.[90] Given that White and Epston conceived their theory by turning away from all the prevailing theoretical and practical views informed by individualism, the narrative approach has the profound potential to recover human beings' relationality.[91]

---

90. Ibid., 5.

91. Madigan, *Narrative Therapy*, 12.

CHAPTER 6

Narratives: Powerful Instruments for Pastoral Practices

6.1. Introduction

IN THIS CHAPTER, I explore human beings' inseparable relationship with metaphors and discuss the roles of metaphors in light of their two functions, which are called "highlighting" and "hiding." Metaphors have the power to structure our ways of understanding, behaving, and living. Thus, the implications of metaphorical changes are substantial, not only for individuals, but also for academic disciplines and churches as a whole. I will explicate the potential of the metaphor of narratives for pastoral practices for never-married single women in terms of enabling these women to become authors of their own lives. To do so, I will describe what narrative therapy is. Drawing on a number of pastoral theologians who have put narrative theory into conversation with the field of pastoral care and counseling, I will look into ways in which narrative pastoral practices empower never-married single women to become authors of their lives instead of letting the dominant narratives rule over them, including the metaphor of "family," which, in the Korean church, becomes a defining plot for never-married single women.

6.2. Why Metaphors?

In their classic book, *Metaphors We Live By* (1980), George Lakoff and Mark Johnson investigate how human beings' lives have been permeated with countless metaphors. They reveal that metaphors are not additional poetic elements in our daily lives. Rather, metaphors are inseparable parts of being human. Think about expressions like "the world is my oyster," "life is a bowl of cherries," and "a sea of grief." Besides these, there are numerous metaphorical expressions in human languages. Referring to symbols as the smallest units of metaphor, Combs and Freedman echo Lakoff and Johnson noting that "words are in and of themselves symbols of experience."[1] Human beings' lives are replete with countless metaphors.

What grabs my attention is that these ubiquitous metaphors in our languages have a substantial impact on our thoughts and actions. Lakoff and Johnson maintain that metaphors govern our everyday functioning, down to the most mundane details: structuring what we perceive, how we get around in the world, and how we relate to other people.[2] They illustrate how a metaphor can govern the detailed structures of our everyday realities, showing how the metaphor of war is used in relation to arguments, as in the following examples:

> Your claims are *indefensible*.
> He *attacked every weak point* in my argument.
> His criticisms were *right on target*.
> I *demolished* his argument.
> I've never *won* an argument with him.
> You disagree? Okay, *shoot*!
> If you use the *strategy*, he'll *wipe you out*.
> He *shot down* all of my arguments.[3]

Just these simple enumerations of daily expressions regarding an argument help me realize the strong propensity for descriptions of an argument to rely heavily on the concept of battle.

Based on this metaphor of battle or war, it has been natural for me to perceive the other party of a debate as an opponent. When I think about this battle-oriented understanding of an argument, people's hostile attitudes

---

1. Combs and Freedman, *Symbol, Story, and Ceremony*, xv.
2. Lakoff and Johnson, *Metaphors We Live by*, 3.
3. Ibid., 4.

during a debate make sense. Lakoff and Johnson invite their readers to envision "a culture where an argument is viewed as a dance, the participants are seen as performers, and the goal is to perform in a balanced and aesthetically pleasing way."[4] People in such a culture would experience arguments very differently from people whose culture understood argument as a war. What an intriguing invitation to imagine!

This re-visioning of the nature of arguments reminds me of a recent exchange I had with a female student in a master's degree program at my school. She expressed how happy she is to defeat everyone on campus, even students in Ph.D. programs, every time she has a chance to debate them, especially about philosophy. She proudly remarked, "There is nobody who knows more than I do." (Alas!) Not being able to join her celebratory mood over her victory, later that day I felt sorry for her way of perceiving arguments merely in terms of winning and losing. To me, debate is more about arriving at mutual understanding or enlarging one's horizon of understanding by listening to others' different perspectives.

Even though I felt sorry for this student's limited view of debate, it did not occur to me that it might be the metaphor of war that predominantly structures her ways of perceiving debate. Lakoff and Johnson's invitation throws some lights on my frustration. Of course, there might be additional reasons for her specific ways of seeing and behaving. Yet, it is very plausible that the metaphor of war is one of the major operating factors in her epistemology that results in her social attitude toward debate. If she were to approach debate with her colleagues on campus in light of the metaphor of dance or of a cooperative game, her approach would be very different. The metaphors of dance or game would structure her to perceive the other party in a more pleasant or cooperative way.

Metaphors structure our ways of understanding and lead us to perceive and interpret concepts in particular ways. Gergen's view of various forms of negotiated understanding, so-called "descriptions" and "explications," harmonizes with Lakoff and Johnson's explanation of the function of metaphors in our lives. As Gergen points out the critical significance of forms of negotiated understanding in social life, he further denotes the vital role of a range of descriptions and explications in terms of structuring social patterns.[5] For example, there are associated actions expected with simple greetings such as, "Hi," and "How are you?" Socially constructed

4. Ibid., 5.
5. Gergen, "The Social Constructionist Movement in Modern Psychology," 268.

descriptions of things entail certain codes of behavior as we interact with others.

When I was young, my father used to scold me for acting like a tomboy saying, "It is not how a girl is supposed to be." My father encouraged certain lines of action based on conventional descriptions of femininity that he preferred. Trying to be a good daughter, I made an effort, albeit frustrated, to become acquainted with a certain pattern of demeanors that would meet the conventional descriptions of women as quiet, submissive, and reserved. In fact, Gergen's concept of socially constructed descriptions corresponds to the concept of sociocultural narratives addressed in Chapter 3 in terms of having power over our ways of being and thinking.

As negotiated understandings of realities, entrenched metaphors and images in our daily lives have a very similar function. This aspect of metaphors becomes clear in light of Lakoff and Johnson's description of what a metaphor is: "the essence of metaphor is understanding and experiencing one kind of thing in terms of another."[6] That is, an argument is not a war. Yet, the metaphor of war causes persons to understand and experience arguments in correlation to war. As negotiated understandings of realities, metaphors are influential vehicles for structuring people's ways of perceiving things and acting accordingly.

Along with this influential role of metaphor, Lakoff and Johnson point out the reverse side of metaphors' functioning. Whereas they phrase the former function as "highlighting," they name the latter function of metaphor, "hiding."[7] While a metaphor of a concept forms our perception of the concept by highlighting certain aspects, this function inadvertently yet necessarily entails hiding other aspects of the concept that are incongruent with the metaphor. As people understand debate through the metaphor of battle, the other aspects of debate get screened out from people's ways of perceiving debate. Highlighting and hiding are the two functions of the same coin called "metaphor."

These highlighting and hiding functions of metaphors do not circumscribe the parameter merely at the individual level. The impact of metaphors is evident both in our understanding of God and in academic disciplines as well. Keenly aware of the devastating influence of traditional metaphors for God, Sallie McFague, in *Models of God* (1987), offers new alternative metaphors of God as mother, lover, and friend in order to correct the distorted

6. Lakoff and Johnson, *Metaphors We Live by*, 5.
7. Ibid., 10.

relationship between God and the world based on the metaphors of God as king, ruler, lord, master, and governor. Whereas the primary metaphors in the tradition are hierarchical, imperialistic, and dualistic, MacFague hopes to lay a relational foundation based on mutuality, shared responsibility, reciprocity, and love between God and the world through her new metaphors.[8] Further, what someone thinks about "church," that person's ecclesiology, has traditionally been framed by a few metaphorical understandings. In his book, *Images of the Church* (1960), Paul Minear identifies four major clusters of images of the church in the New Testament: "the people of God," "the new creation," "the fellowship in faith," and "the body of Christ."

The influence of metaphors is also substantial in the field of psychology. When traditional Freudian psychoanalysis theory considers the therapist to be a "blank sheet," the therapist's subjectivity (countertransference) is not construed in a positive way, and is instead referred to as "unconscious distortions in the helper's perception due to unresolved internal issues usually rooted in early childhood."[9] Psychoanalysis programs try to train counselors to set aside their subjectivity while they are engaged in any therapeutic relationship. Just like the idea that surgeons benefit their patients most when they keep their emotional distance, counselors are admonished to maintain emotional neutrality for the sake of their clients.

The metaphor of "repairman" from first-order cybernetics aligns with this train of thought, in spite of the prevailing archeological metaphor from the traditional Freudian framework. The following remarks from Freedman and Combs underscore the hiding function of metaphors from traditional Freudian psychoanalysis and first-order cybernetics: "As the idea of individual minds in individual bodies once limited our ability to conceptualize and work with mind as an interpersonal phenomenon in family systems, the idea of 'family systems' now can limit our ability to think about the flow of ideas in our larger culture."[10] These hidden areas have come to light through metaphors that have attracted second-order cybernetic thinkers.

Turning away from the metaphors of system and structure that first-order cybernetics relies on, second-order cybernetics brings humility to the field, acknowledging the unavoidable humanness of therapists through more ecosystemic-epistemology-oriented metaphors such as "coevolution" and "co-creation." On this ground, I consider the shift from first-order

8. McFague, *Models of God*, 19.
9. Cooper-White, *Shared Wisdom*, 5.
10. Freedman and Combs, *Narrative Therapy*, 2.

cybernetics to second-order cybernetics a metaphorical alteration. As I reflect on shifts within the field of family therapy, metaphors are not trivial matters. Instead, metaphors are powerful instruments that construct not only individuals but also academic disciplines in a particular way. I find this aspect of metaphors underlying the reasons why pastoral theologians, starting with Anton T. Boisen, have proposed numerous images and metaphors in relation to pastoral practices.

Boisen, the founder of Clinical Pastoral Education, suggested the well-known image of the "living human document," which acknowledged the depth of every human being. Boisen's image has been revisited by Gerkin (1984) and Miller-McLemore (1996). There are a number of images in addition to this one that illumine who a pastoral caregiver is and what the field of pastoral care and counseling is about, such as Seward Hiltner's metaphor of the solicitous shepherd, Henri Nouwen's "wounded healer," and Karen Hanson's image of the midwife. In fact, Robert Dykstra's book, *Images of Pastoral Care* (2005), introduces a number of images from Boisen to the late 1990s in the field of pastoral care and counseling.

It is true that various metaphors have contributed to revitalizing, expanding, and also complicating understandings of ministry and pastoral practices. Dykstra holds that pastoral images nurture "a richer sense of pastoral self-understanding, identity and integrity."[11] Images and metaphors shed light on our understandings of who we are as pastoral caregivers. In addition, images and metaphors have an influential power in terms of what we do as a field when a majority of scholars in the field are persuaded by certain theologians' rationales for certain images and metaphors. Images and metaphors can enlarge our understanding of our personal identities as caregivers as well as the identity of the field, creating a fresh way to rethink its functioning.

For example, the image of Boisen's living human document constructed the field to focus on individuals' psyches, acknowledging that such a document is as valuable as scripture and traditions. On the other hand, the metaphor of "web" used by Miller-McLemore (1993), Patton (1993), and Pamela Couture (1995) has invited the field to reconsider practices of care to take into consideration the inextricably interwoven webs of people's lives. The metaphor of web has uncovered what has been concealed by the metaphor of the living human document. In her recent book, *Christian Theology in Practice: Discovering a Discipline* (2012), Miller-McLemore

---

11. Dykstra, *Images of Pastoral Care*, 13.

proposes the metaphor of "living document within the web" in order to remedy the problems that the metaphor of web has overlooked by retrieving the worth of Boisen's metaphor.[12] Given the significance of prevailing images and metaphors upon individuals and the discipline, more endeavors to offer alternative metaphors and images are justified.

In this vein, I welcome the metaphor of "narratives" as I envision pastoral practices for never-married women in this postmodern age. Since prevailing metaphors, as negotiated understandings of reality, promote certain modes of behavior, they can keep us from seeing alternative ways and inadvertently obscure other dimensions of reality. As Gergen aptly grasps, "to alter description and explanation is . . . to threaten certain actions and invite others."[13] Changing metaphors has political implications because such changes challenge the status quo and invite people to think and perceive things from a different perspective. Here lie the reasons why I want to engage the metaphor of narratives to address pastoral practices with never-married single women. In fact, the potentials of the metaphor of narratives get more evident with comprehension of what narrative therapy is.

Drawing on a few pastoral scholars who have pioneered the construction of pastoral practices based on narrative therapy, such as Bidwell, Coyle, Lester, Neuger, and Scheib, I find the narrative approach useful for empowering never-married single women to generate preferred stories of their lives, so they can eventually re-author their own unique stories instead of merely conforming to dominant sociocultural narratives about who they should be. The metaphor of narratives can shed light on the areas concealed in darkness before.

Specifically, it is my aim to construct pastoral practices based on the metaphor of narratives in order to invite both caregivers and careseekers to a more decentralized model of care. Given the hierarchical structure between caregivers (ministers) and careseekers (laypersons), especially during a time when "a psychological model has been at the center of our understanding of the pastor's relationship with parishioners," I consider it important to raise an awareness of power dynamics between caregivers and careseekers.[14] Power has to be understood in terms of mutuality. Caregivers need to focus on ways to empower careseekers so that careseekers

---

12. Miller-McLemore, *Christian Theology in Practice*, 51.
13. Gergen, "The Social Constructionist Movement in Modern Psychology," 268.
14. Wimberly, *Recalling Our Own Stories*, 6.

eventually reclaim their authority over their own lives and are able to reauthor their stories.

6.3. Why the Metaphors of Narratives?

When I first heard the term, *narrative therapy*, it grabbed my attention because of my interest in stories. At first, I just sensed that narrative therapy must be something related to stories. I know few people who do not like stories. As a preacher, I have experienced the power of stories to garner people's attention and have them listen to me. Most preachers would relate to the power of stories for invigorating even sleepy congregants' imaginations to engage a Scripture text that is dull and flat. In addition, as a pastoral caregiver, I was intrigued by peoples' stories that enabled me more fully to understand what Boisen meant by the expression, "living human document," which I ran into for the first time in my M.Div. courses. It was people's stories that led me to extend my enrollment in a one-year residency CPE program to two years.

When I first encountered the term, *living human document*, I liked it because of its somewhat poetic description of the depths of human beings. As I was exposed to countless profound stories from everyday people at the hospital where I did my residency, however, I understood this term at a whole different level, realizing the power of stories over the storytellers. Most of all, I was astonished by the fact that everyone has stories to tell, regardless of their ages, educational levels, ethnic backgrounds, or socioeconomic statuses. When I introduced myself as a chaplain on the floor, people reeled off their very distinctive stories, which were neither rehearsed nor repeated to anyone else. I have had a deep gratitude for their show of trust in telling me, a total stranger, their stories and allowing me to walk their journeys with them. Without a doubt, people's stories turned my world upside down. My ways of understanding Christianity, the world, and God have been substantially altered because of people's stories.

Secondly, it struck me that how people framed their stories seemed much more important than what exactly happened. I heard stories that were beyond anything I had ever imagined could really happen in people's lives, and I was amazed at how resilient human beings can be. Some stories were too tragic even to fathom. Nonetheless, people's experiences of those stories were not the same. Whereas some people seemed to be seized by the weight of their stories, there were those who surprisingly celebrated their unfathomably painful stories. Without any theoretical support, I pondered these contrasting responses, wondering what would be the reasons for the resiliency of those who engaged the heartbreaking events of their lives in a more positive way. How do people come to own their stories and not the opposite, have their stories own them? However, after I left the hospital, this question was forgotten and remained unresolved as I started my Ph.D. program and became busy with other subjects.

When I was first introduced to narrative theory through Lester's *Hope in Pastoral Care and Counseling* (1995) and Stephen Madigan's *Narrative Therapy* (2010) during my clinical training with Duane Bidwell at The Clinebell Institute for Pastoral Counseling and Psychotherapy, my interest in stories was reawakened. I was thrilled to find that there is an academic discussion called "narrative theory." Not only that, the field of pastoral care and counseling has engaged with this emerging field to propose pastoral practices based on the metaphor of narratives. Beyond learning that narrative therapy is about relating to stories, I have become riveted by the theoretical foundations behind it: text analogy and poststructural ideas. I will explicate the promising aspects of the metaphor of narratives for the current study in light of the text analogy and then explain poststructural ideas.

The origin of the metaphor of narratives can be found in the text analogy: White denoted the text analogy as "the broadest of the recent refigurations of social theory."[15] White drew the expression, "the refiguration of social thought," from Clifford Geertz, who used it to refer to a shift among social scientists in the early 1980s.[16] Geertz pointed out social scientists' inclination by the early 1980s to relinquish reductionist thought. Instead, they turned to analogies which came from "the contrivances of cultural performance [rather] than those of physical manipulation."[17] Geertz's concept of the refiguration of social thought is well articulated by the line, "the instruments of reasoning are changing and society is less and less represented as an elaborate machine or a quasi-organism and more as a serious game, a sidewalk drama, or a behavioral text."[18]

As I found in my literature review presented in Chapter 3, a corresponding phenomenon happened within the field of family therapy. Along with family therapists, many social scientists have started comprehending

---

15. White, "The Process of Questioning," 40.
16. Geertz, *Local Knowledge*, 19.
17. Ibid., 22.
18. Ibid., 23.

social realities through different analogies or metaphors (I consider metaphors and analogies interchangeable concepts). White and Epston incorporated the text analogy, understanding people's lives and relationships "in terms of reading and writing texts."[19] Developing their therapeutic model based on one of the new analogies employed by social scientists, White and Epston remembered that "the analogies that we employ determine our examination of the world: the questions we ask about events, the realities we construct, and the 'real' effects experienced by those parties to the inquiry."[20]

White and Epston demonstrate their alignment with social scientists' conclusion that "we cannot have direct knowledge of the world, ... what persons know of life they know through 'lived experience,'" by employing the metaphors of *text*, *reader*, and *writer*.[21] Human beings discover meanings as they articulate their own lived experiences through stories. This is what White and Epston mean when they remark that "in order to make sense of our lives and to express ourselves, experience must be 'storied' and it is this storying that determines the meaning ascribed to experience."[22] As we tell our stories, we ascribe certain meanings to those stories. However, we do not tell all that has happened to us. Instead, we pick and choose meaningful events and share them, not necessarily in a linear manner.

According to Karen Scheib, the point at which one begins or the story one chooses to tell when invited to share something about oneself often reveals a theme central to one's identity.[23] When I asked my interviewees to tell me about themselves, they briefly told their stories chronologically from birth to their current statuses. Yet, coming to the United States was like a watershed for all of them because they all chose to tell their stories centered around their emigration to the U.S. Such a narrative theme, which plays a major role in a person's sense of self, is what Lester calls "a core narrative."[24] People construct meanings out of the stories they tell about who they are and what their lives are about. For this reason, I think Scheib is right on target when she builds a conversation between narrative theory and social constructionism. Just as social constructionist ideas presuppose

19. White and Epston, *Narrative Means to Therapeutic Ends*, 9.
20. Ibid., 5.
21. Ibid., 9.
22. Ibid., 9–10.
23. Scheib, *Challenging Invisibility*, 57.
24. Lester, *Hope in Pastoral Care and Counseling*, 30.

a socially constructed reality, narrative therapy understands that human beings participate in a meaning-making process through the stories they choose to tell.

David Polkinghorne's definition of *narrative* rightly captures this dimension of it. He defines narrative "as a meaning-making device whose individual components are organized into a coherent whole."[25] The meanings of people's lives can be different depending on the stories they choose to tell. In light of this aspect of storied experiences, I have discovered some clues regarding the power of stories over the storytellers, and I have found the words to articulate my unresolved question about how storytellers come to own their stories. Specifically, the following comment by White shed some light on my previous quandary: "Thus we could investigate the benefit of defining a therapy of 'literary merit' in which the therapist's greatest gift to persons seeking therapy is to help them become their own writers."[26] I was fascinated by the idea that therapy can help people become the writers of their own lives. It is my hope for this research to find ways to empower never-married Korean Christian women to become authors of their own lives rather than live into the stories written by their churches and cultures. This is a creative way to look at acts of caring and helping.

The metaphor of authoring one's life has altered my way of understanding therapy and the caregiving role of a pastoral counselor. It is not about fixing and correcting. Instead, it is more about honoring the agency that people seeking therapy already have within them. I have learned that this distinctive aspect is related to narrative therapy's approach of distinguishing a problem from the person with the problem. Within the narrative paradigm, "the problem becomes the problem, and then the person's relationship with the problem becomes the problem."[27] I will elaborate on this later when I discuss externalizing problems. For now, I would like to focus on one of the strengths of the metaphor of narratives that undergirds White's idea of helping people become the writers of their own lives.

What intrigues me from White's idea is, if people become writers of their own lives, it means they have power over their own stories and their stories do not have power over them. I am intentional in appropriating a "power over" metaphor rather than a "power with" or "power for" metaphor here in order to stress people's distance from their stories. For me, this

---

25. Polkinghorne, *Narrative Knowing and the Human Sciences*, 58.
26. White, "The Process of Questioning," 40.
27. White and Epston, *Narrative Means to Therapeutic Ends*, 40.

is particularly critical given the situation never-married single women face. Considering the influence of the marriage and family discourse, which robs people of the ability to imagine alternative ways of being, sociocultural narratives become the authors of never-married women's stories, not the never-married women themselves. One of my interviewees' experiences is relevant to this point:

> Some people around me tell me that my single life is not what God intended for people. It hurts because they seem to tell me that my life is not biblical, despite my love for God and God's love for me. . . . I do not recall receiving a direct teaching that "people should get married" from my church or my parents. But what we see is often more important than what we are taught. People do things, not based on what they learn, but based on what they see. When all church programs are designed for married couples and families, marriage and family become the norm. Automatically, my way of being is perceived as abnormal. . . . The thought, "I should get married," has seemed to have been carved on me because of the absence of diverse ways of living in my faith communities.

Other interviewees also shared the pressures placed on them because of the marriage and family discourse, regardless of their interest in following its norms. Therefore, I find it vital to empower never-married single women to become the authors of their own lives. The metaphor of narratives suits such a mission. Since it is a pivotal concept for my study, let us examine this idea in more detail.

White borrowed the metaphor of narrative from psychologist Jerome Bruner. In his book, *Actual Minds, Possible Worlds* (1986), Bruner suggests two modes of thought, the narrative mode and the paradigmatic mode (or logico-scientific mode). These two modes of thought can be understood as "a good story and a well-formed argument," respectively.[28] While both of them can be used to persuade others, according to Bruner, "what they convince *of* is fundamentally different: arguments convince one of their truth, stories of their lifelikeness."[29] One of the shortcomings of the former mode of thought is that it leads people into certain kinds of blindness through washing away stories. For instance, scientists can overlook certain biased practices involved in research because of their premises, conclusions, and observations that are based on their specific type of training. Therefore,

---

28. Bruner, *Actual Minds, Possible Worlds*, 11.
29. Ibid.

Bruner argues for "the imaginative application of the narrative mode," which eventually leads to "good stories, gripping drama, [and] believable (though not necessarily 'true') historical accounts."[30]

Further, Bruner discusses stories of literary merit that call upon readers to become writers who construct a virtual text of their own by responding to the stories.[31] Bruner continues, "the actual text needs the subjunctivity that makes it possible for a reader to create a world of his own. . . . I believe that the writer's greatest gift to a reader is to help him become a writer."[32] What Bruner means by "subjunctivity" is some flexibility that allows multifaceted interpretations to play a significant role in the creation of a reader's own world. In other words, if I read a novel, even if I know it is fiction, I become excited, sad, and even tearful, as if I were the protagonist or another character in the novel. I create a world of my own that might not be the same as the world that my friend would create as she reads the same novel. This is possible because of the subjunctivity a writer offers to readers.

In contrast to the pragmatic mode of thought, which simply seeks to find conclusive or inconclusive results, with no flexibility, narratives allow a more complex and often ambiguous mode of thought. As I dwell on Bruner's concept of subjunctivity, I am reminded of White and Epston's remark: "Stories are full of gaps which persons must fill in order for the story to be performed."[33] I think improvisation during a performance can be a good example of "filling in the gaps." A play is replete with gaps that actors and actresses fill as they perform it. Hence, White and Epston think these gaps call up the lived experiences and imaginations of persons. What White and Epston mean by "gaps" is a parallel concept to Bruner's subjunctivity. In order to help readers become writers who create their own worlds, stories need to have gaps. It is readers who are responsible for filling in gaps through performing the stories they read. Yet, there is no blueprint for how to do this. It all depends on readers' preferences.

Drawing on Bruner, White substituted "therapists" for "writers." The greatest gift of therapy is to empower people seeking help to become writers of their lives. I want to encourage pastoral caregivers to regard their role in this light. To provide this assistance, it is necessary for pastoral caregivers

---

30. Ibid., 13.

31. White translated Bruner's "stories of literary merit" into "a therapy of literary merit" as the subtitle of his article, "The Process of Questioning."

32. Bruner, *Actual Minds, Possible Worlds*, 37.

33. White and Epston, *Narrative Means to Therapeutic Ends*, 13.

to empower people seeking help to create some distance from their past experiences so they can consider what kinds of stories are woven into their core stories. Further, it is an important task for caregivers to ask new questions to help careseekers interpret their texts, i.e., their life events, from a different perspective.

Pointing out the usefulness of careful and curious questioning for finding alternative stories, Bidwell specifies that the function of such questioning is to challenge and deconstruct the dominant stories.[34] Pastoral caregivers need to formulate questions to empower never-married single women to discover the ways in which marriage and family discourse affects their sense of self. These questions will guide careseekers to create their own worlds in which they will be born into writers of their lives. In fact, this questioning process is a prerequisite for arriving at the re-authoring phase. This approach is, to me, fertile ground where pastoral practices can retrieve their life-affirming function for people at the margins, including never-married single women. Before I engage with the re-authoring strategy in relation to externalizing internalized problems, I want to explicate the other theoretical background of narrative theory: poststructural ideas.

6.4. Finding the Concealed Stars

Poststructural ideas represented by the French philosophers Michel Foucault and Jacques Derrida provide narrative theory with a philosophical ground. The postmodern epistemological ground on which narrative theory stands has drawn my attention because narrative theory is committed to align with part of what I believe is God's aim, which is "to decolonize, diversify and promote counter-hegemonic social conditions."[35] This aspect of God is germane to the reason why I chose to engage with narrative theory for pastoral practices for never-married single women, as I will explain.

Narrative theory critiques existing psychodynamic theory, viewing therapy as a social process instead of a set of intra-psychic processes. Hence, John McLeod considers narrative therapy postpsychological.[36] The following encapsulation from Madigan of what narrative therapy is not points to what narrative therapy is about:

---

34. Bidwell, *Empowering Couples*, 46.
35. Lartey, *Postcolonializing God*, xiii.
36. McLeod, "Narrative Thinking and the Emergence of Postpsychological Therapies," 202.

> Narrative therapy is neither essentialist, structural, psychodynamic, systemic, nor based on individualizing principles of the self. Nor does narrative theory advocate the use of developmental models, theories of the individualized self, the use of psychological testing, nor the use of texts such as the Diagnostic and Statistical Manual of Mental Disorders . . . Nor does the practice readily turn to pharmaceuticals.[37]

Repudiating the objective underlying structures that could explain human conditions, narrative therapy acknowledges the probability of numerous interpretations about persons and problems based on "a central poststructural tenet . . . that we, as persons, are multistoried."[38] From narrative therapists' perspective, human beings are multilayered.

Understanding human beings as multifaceted corresponds to the postcolonializing aspect of God in that "postcolonializing activities . . . promote multi-dimensional discourses and practices."[39] A postcolonializing God likely understands human beings' identities as fluid. In fact, our stories can be told in numerous ways, depending on where we stand to perceive them. Thus, Edward Bruner is right when he argues that "life experience is richer than discourse," warning people not to confuse anthropological stories about Indians with concrete existence or "real" facts.[40] Instead, he states that "my focus is on our talk about Indians, not on Indian life itself."[41] It is his acknowledgement that there is a much bigger Indian reality his anthropological stories cannot include.

Stories and our understandings of ourselves always have things left out. When people are robbed of the vision to see this multistoried side of their life stories, they may become stuck in their fixation on a particular story. Labels based on the *Diagnostic and Statistical Manual of Mental Disorders* (DSM) in psychiatric practice are typical examples that deny the multistoried aspect of people's selves. Madigan's anecdote about his client Tom illustrates how narrative therapists strive to explore multistoried selves, not accepting a diagnosis from the DSM as part of the permanent identity of a client.

---

37. Madigan, *Narrative Therapy*, xvii.
38. Ibid., 12.
39. Lartey, *Postcolonializing God*, xvii.
40. Bruner, "Ethnography as Narrative," 143.
41. Ibid.

Madigan's client, Tom, "a 66-year-old White, middle-class, abled-bodied, married, heterosexual male," was referred to him with the label of "suicidal and depressed" after a local psychiatric hospital tried "everything" they could, including 40 electroconvulsive therapies within a 12-month period.[42] Madigan received Tom's six-pound hospital case file diagnosing Tom as having a chronic major depressive disorder. However, he refused to accept the staff's "expert" knowledge about Tom as to who Tom really was.

Instead, Madigan's therapeutic conversations with Tom sought to separate Tom from the totalized "chronic major depression" identity description that had been paralyzing him and to empower him to remember abilities and aspects of his life that the identification of the problem in this way had helped him forget.[43] (I will explain the strategy of externalizing internalized problems later in this chapter in relation to re-authoring stories.) By Week 12 of narrative therapy, Tom was able to function better than normal without additional medication. Madigan's report of Tom's personal sharing regarding the therapy is as follows:

> Tom had stated plainly that he had experienced a lot of appreciation, compassion, and listening during our talks and through the influx of therapeutic letters from his community of concern. He also stated that he liked the way we stepped "outside the box" to get a better understanding of his relationship with the problem and how we reviewed aspects and stories of his life that could not be explained through the problem and the hospital's definition of him.[44]

I think Tom's personal experience of narrative therapy reflects what narrative therapy is committed to. Madigan's approach enabled Tom to gain distance from his own problem by stepping out of the box that the medical staff had created. Labels given to people by experts of psychological knowledge or by dominant sociocultural discourses can play such a strong role in people's lives that they are blinded to their true identities. Unless people are empowered to find alternative ways to define themselves, they are prone to believe the naming that is given to them without question. This is the hegemonic power that a totalitarian theory has over us, and it is against God's preference for diversity.

42. Madigan, *Narrative Therapy*, 5.
43. Ibid., 7.
44. Ibid., 8.

Therefore, narrative-oriented caregivers need to act "to highlight and undermine dominant cultural knowledges which act to specify, classify, and subjugate a client's identity as fixed."[45] Labels such as "bipolar" and "chronic depression" inhibit exploration of people's multistoried selves. Further, socially constructed terms like "spinster" or the Korean term, "nocheonyu (老處女)," for never-married single women prevent women from seeing other possible selves. I find Robert Kegan's metaphor of a constellation of stars in the sky illuminating to this inquiry. Noting that "it is we who are doing the constellating, not the stars or the heavens,"[46] Kegan points out that myriad stars have been overlooked because of the constructed constellations consisting of particular stars.

It is not stars that have been connected to one another in order to constitute constellations such as the Big Dipper, Pegasus, or Scorpius. Rather, human beings have connected a few stars which would be far away from each other in a three-dimensional space and transposed them onto two-dimensional shapes as if they were intrinsically related to one another. People see the Big Dipper night after night, not because these are the only stars in the sky, but because science classes have taught them to notice it. In other words, authoritative teachings screen out countless other stars, keeping people from seeing them. I think Suzanne Coyle's concept of "a solid one-plot story" that cuts off new stories to become a part of people's faith stories relates to this.[47]

Instead of seeking multi-leveled stories, according to Coyle, "We believe . . . that the one story we have told for so many years is more important than the small stories that try to push through the cracks in the wall of perfection."[48] Pastoral practices rooted in the metaphor of narratives seek to enable careseekers to find concealed stars, these small stories of themselves, so that these stars can be woven into their life stories and their understandings of who they are can be enlarged and transformed. In Foucault's terminology, these concealed stars are "local knowledges" that are often silenced by dominant discourses because they do not fit these discourses' criteria of acceptability.[49] Unless there is a nudge to notice multifaceted stories, people

---

45. Madigan, "The Politics of Identity," 50.
46. Kegan, *In over Our Heads*, 206.
47. Coyle, *Re-Storying Your Faith*, 5.
48. Ibid.
49. Madigan, *Narrative Therapy*, 45.

are prone to live out certain aspects of their stories without knowing alternative ways to frame their stories. According to Madigan,

> Narrative therapy's approach to the self stretches out beyond the more popular and/or generalized accounts of who persons are (e.g., dominant and/or individualized categories of personhood) and of who the person is stated or labeled to be by the expert of psychological knowledge.[50]

Since narrative theory is opposed to an essentialist view of self, narrative therapists strive to empower clients to construct alternative and preferred stories. To do so, Bidwell stresses the significance of looking into the margins, stating that "alternative wisdom resides at the margins," silenced and unnoticed because of the power and volume of those of dominant stories.[51] For example, Bidwell encourages caregivers to explore exceptions to the difficulties that careseekers face as one way to identify alternative wisdom. It is important for caregivers to remember that "hidden wisdom often lurks unseen in these problem-free spaces" in order to empower careseekers to find their concealed stars.[52] To accomplish this, caregivers need to have careseekers separate themselves from their problems. That is the topic that I turn to now.

6.5. Re-Constellations

Separating a person from a problem is grounded on a narrative philosophy that refuses to locate problems inside people.[53] Externalizing the internalized problem is a strategy initiated by White in the early 1980s. According to White, it is "an approach to therapy that encourages persons to objectify and, at times, to personify the problems that they experience as oppressive."[54] A good example of this strategy is articulated in White's article, "Pseudo-Encopresis: From Avalanche to Victory, from Vicious to Virtuous Cycles" (1984). Disagreeing with the approach of traditional psychoanalysis to associate the reason for a child's encopresis with an ambivalent or intrusive mother, White invented a new diagnosis of "pseudo-

---

50. Ibid., 4–5.
51. Bidwell, *Empowering Couples*, 46.
52. Ibid., 47.
53. Denborough, *Retelling the Stories of Our Lives*, 27.
54. White and Epston, *Narrative Means to Therapeutic Ends*, 38.

encopresis."⁵⁵ White signified that this diagnosis is given to "a child who presents as a chronic soiler and where this soiling has persisted despite various attempted solutions, but is not caused by ambivalent and intrusive mothers."⁵⁶ Then he compared the major experiences of encopretic children and their parents.

Whereas the characteristic experiences of parents of encopretic children are "defeat, helplessness, impotence, hopelessness, despair, and frustration," White identified the main experience of children as "the increasing domination of the symptoms."⁵⁷ In the face of their child's struggle, parents tended to accuse themselves of being incapable of fulfilling their roles as parents. The children had lost their control over the problem. The conclusion that White arrived at from his observation is that "all family members within this group were simultaneously experiencing oppression."⁵⁸ A child's soiling habit affected all family members in an oppressive way. White incorporated the externalizing strategy in order to empower these families to relate differently to the problem.

Specifically, White encouraged a child, six-year-old Nick, and his parents, Sue and Ron, to separate the problem from the child by giving the problem a name, "the sneaky poo."⁵⁹ The following questions that White asked demonstrate what this strategy is about:

> "Are you more the boss over the sneaky poo or is it more the boss over you?"; "How often dose the sneaky poo have its way with you compared to how often you have your way with the poo?"; "How often can you put it where you want to?"; . . . "Who should be the boss?"; "Do you want to stand up to the sneaky poo and have your way with it or would it be best to completely give in and let your sneaky poo reign over you and your parents?"; "Do you want to carry the poo off or have it carry you off?"⁶⁰

By locating the problem outside of the child, the child, who had previously been identified as the problem, was no longer the problem. The "sneaky poo" became the problem, and it existed separately from the child. The relationship with the problem was the cause of the problem.

55. White, "Pseudo-Encopresis," 116.
56. Ibid.
57. Ibid.
58. Ibid.
59. Ibid., 118.
60. Ibid.

Using David Denborough's words, if Nick and his parents believe that Nick "*is* the problem, then it becomes very difficult to take action. . . . All Nick can do is to take action against himself."[61] With this narrative point in mind, therefore, Neuger uses "depression" as a noun rather than as an adjective. Neuger's assertion that "women are not depressed—depression and women are not synonymous and depression, even when it has entered a woman's life, doesn't define her,"[62] resonates with White's and Denborough's perspectives. Thus, I believe it is vital that pastoral practices come to reflect this narrative wisdom.

When pastoral caregivers view careseekers separately from their problems, there arises the possibility of empowering careseekers to discern their own power over their problems. As I read White's questions above, I became amused and at the same time liberated by recognizing Nick's power over the sneaky poo that I could not see before. And I ask myself, if I feel liberated as a mere reader, what would this strategy mean for Nick and his parents? Viewing a problem as an external entity to ourselves, we start experiencing it differently.

Thus, it becomes more possible for us to reduce the effects of a problem in our lives and in the lives of others.[63] Considering the reality that all too often people think they are the problem, the implications and possible outcomes of this strategy are priceless. In addition, this process of separating ourselves from our problems makes it possible for us to begin revising our relationships with the problems. White and Epston affirm that "therapy informed by practices associated with the externalizing of problems facilitates the 're-authoring' of lives and relationships."[64] Since it is pivotal for me to empower never-married single women to become writers of their own lives, this re-authoring strategy is where I want pastoral practices to focus. A number of pastoral theologians have already utilized re-authoring/re-storying strategies in pastoral practices. Drawing on their insights, let us look into how this strategy will benefit never-married single women.

Advocating storytelling itself as a spiritual practice, Coyle puts an emphasis on the power of this strategy, titling her book, *Re-storying Your Faith* (2013). I agree with Coyle that, from a feminist perspective, storytelling can be as much a spiritual activity as prayer or Bible study. Considering

---

61. Denborough, *Retelling the Stories of Our Lives*, 25.
62. Neuger, *CounselingWomen*, 168.
63. Denborough, *Retelling the Stories of Our Lives*, 36.
64. White and Epston, *Narrative Means to Therapeutic Ends*, 41–42.

NARRATIVES: POWERFUL INSTRUMENTS FOR PASTORAL PRACTICES

feminists' persistent struggle to empower women to regain the language and voice to name themselves as well as God, storytelling is a potentially powerful spiritual path for never-married single women. In this vein, Neuger considers "coming to voice" as the first step in a narrative-oriented pastoral approach for women, arguing that "women's naming of self, context, and creation is necessary for the full participation of humanity in the ongoing co-creative process with God."[65] I call upon churches to incorporate storytelling as a pastoral practice for those from the margins, including never-married single women.

I think that the devalued status of storytelling practices in comparison to prayer or Bible study is rooted in the modern proclivity to value the logico-scientific mode of thinking more than the narrative mode of thinking. Postmodern pastoral practices need to be designed to overcome this dualistic dichotomy between the narrative and the pragmatic mode of thinking. To do so, it is necessary to encourage people to participate in the process of storytelling in church communities. Given the reality that most congregants in contemporary Korean churches are expected to listen while a few ministers and elders talk, it is crucial for churches to provide never-married single women with a space in which they can articulate their own stories, because I believe "it is the empowerment of hearing oneself speak and learning to believe in the truth of that long-denied voice, language, and narrative" that is so important.[66] This practice will resist the sociocultural narrative that considers never-married women "immature." Instead, it will cultivate a respect for everyone as worthy of telling their stories and being heard. This practice will be an important building block for decentralized communities, which I will describe in the following chapter.

Coyle defines re-storying as "a narrative process by which people intentionally decide which stories they want to develop in order to enrich their life stories and personal identity."[67] What Coyle means by "intentionally" can be understood from the perspective of the multifaceted aspects of human beings' stories I mentioned previously. Since there are always stories and stars screened out from our epistemological sky, both caregivers and careseekers need to be intentional about seeking alternative stories. Unless we become intentional, there is no way out from under the oppressive influence of problem-saturated stories or dominant sociocultural stories.

65. Neuger, *Counseling Women*, 72.
66. Ibid., 68.
67. Coyle, *Re-Storying Your Faith*, 8.

Identifying this phase as "the process of gaining clarity about a narrative created within a patriarchal context," Neuger maintains that gaining clarity needs to follow the therapeutic process of coming to voice.[68] This step would empower people to uncover stories that have been lost and discredited because of deep-rooted patriarchal lies.

In a similar vein, Bidwell identifies re-storying as "an act of resistance."[69] As couples are encouraged to recall stories that contradict the current problem that would separate them, couples become able to discern new dimensions to their existing stories. Bidwell's definition of re-storying succinctly captures human beings' agency to create stories that attribute new meanings to their experiences. White and Epston regard these hidden possibilities as "historical unique outcomes" that can be catalysts to generating performances of new meanings in the present and revising people's problem-saturated stories.[70] Human beings are not powerless in the face of the tyranny of life stories. We have inherent agency to shape our stories by making choices about which stories we will highlight. Pastoral practices need to be designed to empower careseekers to discover this agency, perhaps denied for a long time, within them.

Therefore, Neuger associates the re-authoring strategy with "making choices" in order to "resist and transform the oppressive forces" in women's lives.[71] This phase is critical for bringing about transformation in women's lives along with the previous two steps of coming to voice and gaining clarity. Although Neuger acknowledges the significance of the previous two steps, if there is "no support to make choices in light of the lies overturned and new truths found, . . . no real transformation can occur."[72] Given the commitment of the field of pastoral care and counseling to enhancing people's quality of life, re-storying seems an inevitable step to utilize in pastoral practices.

Rebecca Chopp reinforces the possibility that people can rewrite their lives from a different perspective. She affirms that "each woman and man has the possibility and responsibility to compose her or his life. The women, and the men, cannot or do not have to fit into predetermined narratives or

---

68. Neuger, *Counseling Women*, 129.
69. Bidwell, *Empowering Couples*, 47.
70. White and Epston, *Narrative Means to Therapeutic Ends*, 56.
71. Neuger, *Counseling Women*, 179.
72. Ibid.

cultural myths."[73] Substituting the terms, *re-authoring* and *re-storying* with "the practice of composing" and "narrativity," Chopp argues for the possibility that men and women in our midst can "intentionally create their lives in relation to their culture, their bodies, their individual experiences, and their Christian communities" through narrativity.[74] People are not meant to just follow socioculturally predetermined narratives. Instead, we need to resist and dismantle cultural myths that silence our contradictory experiences. To this end, pastoral practices empower careseekers to claim their own agency to change the myths they have held onto.

Chopp's approach to sociocultural discourses that structure our ways of being as "myths" harmonizes with Edward Wimberly's understanding. Wimberly's aim is to bring about transformation in people's myths—personal, marital-family, and ministry myths—by focusing on re-storying strategies in pastoral practices. In *Recalling Our Own Stories* (1997), Wimberly refers to "the beliefs and convictions that people have about themselves, their relationships with others, their roles in life, and their ministry" as "mythologies."[75] Acknowledging the power of dominant myths to shape our lives through attributing meanings to them, Wimberly upholds the possibility of revising these myths and insists that pastoral counseling consider its core task to be "to reedit, or reauthor our own mythologies."[76] Mythologies are not created in a vacuum. Rather, myths are socially constructed and modified by individuals as they are passed on from generation to generation.

In fact, myths that once appeared permanently fossilized are not only changeable but actually awaiting transformation.[77] Mythologies are alterable, no matter how firm they appear, when we are willing to reframe them, because human lived experiences are much richer than what mythologies capture. Wimberly encourages those who hope to re-author their oppressive myths to risk "sailing beyond current horizons" because "changing convictions and beliefs is a prerequisite to bringing about behavioral transformation."[78] In light of Wimberly, theological imagination may be a worthwhile tool to leverage the process of re-storying. In fact, theological

73. Chopp, *Saving Work*, 30.
74. Ibid., 31.
75. Wimberly, *Recalling Our Own Stories*, 4.
76. Denborough, *Retelling the Stories of Our Lives*, 13.
77. Wimberly, *Recalling Our Own Stories*, 75.
78. Ibid., 76.

imagination is an indispensable factor in the discipline of theology, which deals with a God who is beyond our ability to comprehend through reason alone. As I envision my ideal church, I will engage with my theological imagination.

After re-authoring their lives, people need to come back to their own communities. My interviewees belong to church communities and their own families. I want to introduce one of the findings from my interview analyses in relation to communal support. I found that parents' understandings of their daughters' roles in the world influenced my interviewees' singleness. Throughout the interviews, I was struck by how interviewees' parents responded to them differently than I expected. For the question, "How do your parents respond to your being single?" more than two-thirds of my interviewees provided responses that were very different from my own experience. Whereas pressure from my worried father and close family members affected my decision to put "getting married" on my New Year's resolution list, my interviewees reported experiencing different responses from their parents and close family members about their being single.

Seven out of ten interviewees reported feeling no pressure from their parents to get married. When I first heard Julie (a 35-year-old finance executive) talk about her father's support for her, I was very impressed by his feminist perspective in terms of valuing woman's agency. Julie's father told her, "A female does not necessarily have to get married. Since the conjugal knot is from heaven, do not try to stay in a relationship if it means giving up respect for yourself. Go alone like a rhinoceros' horn." Julie expressed gratitude for her father's encouragement. Kathy (a 34-year-old registered nurse) shared that her mother overtly discouraged Kathy from getting married at a young age. Instead, Kathy was encouraged to put a priority on her dream. As a professor at a local college, Kathy's mother married late and knows how hard it will be for her daughter to be a professional after she gets married.

When I first encountered the response from Julie's father in my second interview, I did not expect to listen to descriptions of similar support from my other interviewees. I assumed that Julie's father must be special for some reason. The interview with Kathy was my third interview. Her mother's encouragement was still refreshing to me. Yet, I thought that Kathy's mother was well educated to have such a view. However, the following interviews helped me realize that most of my interviewees are situated in a different context from mine. Most of my interviewees have been able to pursue their dreams without feeling pressure from their immediate families.

The response from the parents of Angelina (a 38-year-old business owner) resonates with the responses of Julie's father and Kathy's mother. Angelina stated, "My parents have had a lot of expectations for me. They have not expected any less than they do for my older brother because I am a daughter. My parents don't talk much about getting married. They always want me to build myself up as a professional individual first, then get married." When Angelina wanted to come to the United States at age 28, her parents applauded her courage and supported her decision. Along with these three, four other interviewees expressed that their parents do not push them to get married. Two of them were currently enrolled in a Ph.D. program. Analyzing my interviews, I speculated about possible reasons for this shift in parents' views toward their daughters.

Given the age difference of approximately 15 or 20 years from my own father, my interviewees' parents are from a different generation who did not live through the Korean War. Thus, they have had more education. In addition, my interviewees are either only daughters or from two-child families. As I contemplated the particularities of my interviewees' *Sitz im Leben*, I was able to comprehend their parents' support for them. Further, I asked myself, "What if their parents' responses had been different, would my interviewees still be where they currently are now as professional women?' I think they would not be where they are. My answer for this question reassures me of the critical role of communal support for those whose lives are re-storied. Specifically, the effectiveness of the pastoral practice of re-authoring requires communal cooperation.

Although careseekers may decide to re-author their lives from a different perspective and claim a different identity from the ones the dominant cultural sociocultural narratives provide them with, when significant people around them do not accept this new identity as who they really are, I suspect that the newly formed identity will not be able to survive long. Neuger rightly points out, "When important people in the counselee's life assume her former narrative to be defining, it is easy for her to get drawn back into the problem narrative."[79] Re-storying practices require a community as a source of resistance. Here lies the reason why I want to envision a church, a counter-community, where Jesus's radical hospitality supports

---

79. Neuger, *Counseling Women*, 184.

people in the continual re-visioning of their lives and celebrates their new identities.

My research suggests that the metaphor of family in Korean churches becomes a defining plot for never-married singe women. Through the eyes of the church, they begin to live the dominant culture's stories of what it means to be a spinster. This erases other aspects of their lives and identities that contradict this limited and limiting account of who they are in the eyes of the church and in the eyes of God. Narrative therapy helps us see possible alternative understandings of self and resist dominant biases and distorted images regarding never-married single women. I argue for a new metaphor for church that strengthens the preexisting traditional ecclesiology by building a bridge between it and the modern church and that keeps providing these women with a source of resistance by being counter-communities rooted in the divine hospitality incarnated through Jesus' ministry on this earth. I turn to this topic in the next chapter.

Chapter 7

A Vision for Churches

7.1. Introduction

WHAT IS THE CHURCH? Why do I need a vision of the church for my project? Some readers might wonder why a pastoral care and counseling research project would end with a chapter on ecclesiology. Like any other academic area, ecclesiology is too broad a topic to be dealt with in a single chapter. I do not intend to cover the whole issue of ecclesiology here. What I want to do in this concluding chapter, however, is to offer normative and pragmatic proposals using a metaphorical understanding of the church in order to ameliorate the unrecognized oppression under which never-married single women live. With the confirmation of the invisibility of never-married single women through my research partners' lived experiences of involuntary isolation and exclusion within their own church communities, I hope to enhance Korean churches' capabilities to empower never-married single women to become authors of their own lives, providing them with places where they can enact their agency through shared power as well as places that recognize them as valued members of the whole community.

I find single women, never-married single women in particular, at the margins of today's Korean churches. Church programs designed for families, couples, and children demonstrate the absence of sensitivity toward their particularity. Since marriage and family is a taken-for-granted reality, the tyranny of the marriage and family discourse is rarely noticed. In Chapters 5 and 6, I analyzed how the marriage and family discourse can control and limit people's ways of being. In this chapter, I want to illustrate the domination of this discourse in never-married single women's lives by introducing my research partners' voices. I will also offer a metaphorical vision of church as an "*a cappella* choir" that not only speaks to the challenges that today's never-married single women face but also has the potential to enlarge churches' ways of being and relating.

First, I will explain why I am engaging with ecclesiology as I suggest the normative and pragmatic tasks of pastoral practices to resolve the sense of exclusion and isolation in my research partners' lived experiences. Although my research partners' experiences in their church communities are varied, a sense of exclusion and isolation emerged as a common thread. I will offer the metaphor of an *a cappella* choir for church communities, suggesting that they become places where all parts and pitches are regarded as indispensable elements for the whole's harmony. Churches as *a cappella* choirs need to function as counter-communities proposing counter values that challenge culturally embedded negative biases about never-married single women and the cultural myth of a "good" woman. Such work can be done through constructing a more developed theological anthropology that promotes the full humanity of never-married single women. Finally, I will explain the notions of divine hospitality and alterity as concepts that will enable Korean churches to cease the practices of exclusion through the violence of assimilation.

7.2. Ecclesiology and Pastoral Practices

I choose to close this research project by offering a new vision for churches in relation to pastoral practices to resolve practices of exclusion because I find it necessary for several reasons. First, the significance of the role of church communities cannot be emphasized enough for pastoral practices which seek to bring people to wholeness because "to be human is to be constituted by relationships with God and other persons."[1] A community is one of the vital elements for humans' wellbeing. In fact, Jesus' acknowledgement of the significance of community for bringing about healing is evident in a number of places in the Bible. When Jesus healed people, his concern was not merely with the improvement of people's physical conditions; Jesus' healing work expanded to reintegrating healed people into their broader society.

---

1. Scheib, *Challenging Invisibility*, 45.

For instance, after being healed by Jesus, Peter's mother-in-law began serving people (Mk 1:31). According to Pheme Perkins, this indicates that "Jesus' healing restoreher to her social position within the household," because showing hospitality to important guests is a role of honor, not servitude, in Jesus' time.[2] Thus, it is reasonable to conclude that the wellness of Peter's mother-in-law resulted not only from her being released from a high fever but also from the reinstatement of her status within the household.

Another example of Jesus' holistic healing follows this incident. Jesus heals a leper, and after healing the leprosy, Jesus instructs the leper to "show yourself to the priest (Mk 1:44)." Perkins views Jesus' instruction as stemming from his concern that "the leper cannot resume normal associations with other people until a priest has inspected his condition and he has performed the required purification rites."[3] Reintegration into the broader society is as important as the improvement of his physical condition. Jesus knew the power of the role of a broader society for bringing healing to individuals. Thus, it is reasonable for me to deal with the broader contexts in which my research partners are situated.

The second reason a vision for churches is needed from a pastoral perspective comes from one of the characteristics of narrative therapy. Narrative pastoral practices will thrive within a communal form of church as opposed to "the consumer form of church, in which people shop to get their spiritual needs met" in today's era.[4] When people come to church and "pay" for a worship service that meets their spiritual needs and then leave, they become just consumers. Just as no one looks for meaningful connections and relationships at a shopping mall, there is hardly a community in the consumer forms of church. To the contrary, narrative pastoral practices require people to be, not consumers, but active participants. This becomes clear in relation to the function of audiences for imparting meaning in narrative therapy.

Introducing the role of alternative documents, such as awards, trophies, and certificates, as a means to bring in a wider audience for the telling of new stories, White and Epston point out that "the incorporation of a wider readership and the recruitment of an audience contribute not just to the survival and consolidation of new meanings, but also to a revision of

---

2. Perkins, "The Gospel of Mark," 546.
3. Ibid.
4. Gibbs and Bolger, *Emerging Churches*, 99.

the preexisting meanings."⁵ As more people participate in the performance of new identities as audience members, there are more opportunities for newly formed identities to survive. For this reason, when churches are able to employ narrative practices to invite more people to serve as audience members, not only are vital communities created but people's new identities are also given support and a space to flourish. I hope whole church communities become active audiences for never-married single women's performances of their new identities and meanings in their lives.

Lastly, Daniel Izuzquiza calls my attention to the need for a vision of the church in relation to pastoral practices. Upholding Christian communities as "the embodiment of a radical alternative," Izuzquiza asserts the priority of an ecclesiological vision in our struggle for social change.⁶ Social transformation is possible when Christian communities embody a radical alternative to the dominant system. Izuzquiza regards an ecclesiological vision as an indispensable factor in achieving such a goal. Agreeing with him, I want to offer a vision for the church, not only for sustaining individual transformation, but also for enlarging it to the realm of social change. In effect, paradigm shifts that have happened within the field of pastoral care and counseling have been about enlarging the boundaries of care and the effects of this expansion. Pastoral practices that hope to participate in broadening the limits of pastoral practices need to go beyond the dimension of individual salvation and well-being to struggle with a vision for church that aims at bringing "social transformation arising from the presence and permeation of the reign of Christ."⁷ My vision for the church is a powerful means through which pastoral practices can make an impact on the larger human community.

For this reason, I find Scheib's research in *Challenging Invisibility: Practices of Care with Older Women* (2004) valuable in terms of her proposing an ecclesiology where her pastoral practices for aging women are sustained. Through the image of "a widening circle of gracious inclusion," Scheib insists on the necessity of a community where people make an effort to keep broadening the circle of relations in order to deconstruct the marginalization of older women.⁸ She hopes this continuous endeavor to widen the circle will eventually culminate in a community of gracious

---

5. White and Epston, *Narrative Means to Therapeutic Ends*, 191.
6. Izuzquiza, *Rooted in Jesus Christ*, 126–27.
7. Gibbs and Bolger, *Emerging Churches*, 63.
8. Scheib, *Challenging Invisibility*, 47.

inclusion where older women feel a genuine sense of belonging and being heard and respected.

Although Scheib does not articulate the implications of a widening circle of gracious inclusion on the greater human community, I foresee a ripple effect of what an ever-widening circle of gracious inclusion can bring to the broader society when whole church communities participate in expanding their circles of inclusion. This vision for churches has the potential to enrich not only the lives of older women within church communities but also the lives of people in the larger society. Such an ecclesiological vision can be a powerful way to assist the field of pastoral care and counseling to the extent that transformations embodied in people's daily lives can be expanded to social changes. Given church communities' crucial role to maintain revised stories and identities brought about through narrative pastoral practices, I choose to propose a vision for church communities.

I hope my ecclesiological vision sheds some light for Korean churches as they create their futures by endeavoring to provide a space for the kindom on this earth. Although my ecclesiological vision is based on Korean-American, never-married single women's lived experiences, I do not think this necessarily limits the potential influence of my ecclesiological vision to Korean churches. I think that those who hope to dismantle any type of marginalization in faith communities will benefit from it and deepen their understandings regarding divine hospitality, the notion of alterity, and the significance of power distribution. Before articulating my vision for church communities, I would like my readers to listen to my interviewees' voices about their experiences of church communities as never-married single women. My vision for church communities will be more comprehensible in light of their lived experiences.

7.3. Lived Experiences of My Research Partners

What is church for today's never-married single women? Is church a place where never-married single women experience abundant life through a sense of belonging? In order to answer these questions, I will draw on my interviewees' experiences of being single in local Korean churches. But first I would like to share the experience of one of my friends, Rosa (a medical doctor who is nearing retirement), who I initially contacted to talk with about my project and ask if I could interview her. Rosa expressed her regret at not being a suitable person for my project because she has not associated with Korean churches for more than 10 years. Yet, she was willing to share her reasons for leaving a Korean church in a suburban area in New Jersey about 10 years ago.

Since leaving that church, Rosa has attended a megachurch in Manhattan where she feels like she belongs and is respected as a valued member of the congregation. In fact, my conversation with Rosa helped me limit my research to never-married single women from Korean churches, realizing there may be different experiences between those who attend American churches and those who go to Korean churches. Although I acknowledge that not all American churches are like the church Rosa is attending in terms of their efforts to respect various ways of living, embodying a sensitivity to single women in particular, one of the common threads among my interviewees who attend Korean churches is the antithesis of this: they all talked about a sense of exclusion and isolation in their own churches. Their experiences are similar to what Rosa experienced when she was part of a Korean church.

Rosa was attending a small Korean church while she was working at a local hospital as a surgeon. Although I did not ask her why she attended a Korean church during that time, I can assume she found a sense of home there. As a single woman, Rosa felt excluded from time to time, but she was able to let it go. On one Thanksgiving Sunday, however, the worship service was designed for families sitting together. To make things worse, all the families were required to stand in line for their offerings. Each family needed to go to the altar together and then return to their seats. As Rosa stood in the line by herself, she became self-conscious.

She stated, "I couldn't stand 'the gaze' from other families towards my back. I was so embarrassed and humiliated, not because of who I am, but because of who they thought I am. After the service, I decided to leave this church that did not show any sensitivity toward me as a member." One week later, she had a conversation with the senior pastor, letting him know how she felt and her decision to leave the church. Based on other information she gave me, I surmise that this happened in her early fifties or late forties.

As I put Rosa's experience into my own words, I found a clue as to why I had trouble finding a never-married single woman in her fifties attending a Korean church. During the period I was collecting my data, I jotted down a few questions, "Have all Korean females over fifty gotten married? Did they stop going to church at some point? Or are they in the closet?" My contemplation on Rosa's experience leads me to lean toward the second possibility. It seems inhospitality chases never-married single women out of church communities. In addition, Joanna, a 36-year-old lawyer, shared an observation about people's propensity at her church to be biased in their judgment of never-married single women over forty. Joanna interacts with other married people at her church without much trouble. Yet, she finds that "people seem to feel okay about singles until they become over forty. I saw people giving suspicious looks to those never-married single women over forty, though." Apparently, the hospitality of members of Joanna's church extended to single people only until they turned forty.

Rosa's reason for giving up on Korean churches resonates with the remarks of Liz, a 37-year-old pharmacist, who articulated a sense of hopelessness about Korean churches. Liz said, "If I am the only one who doesn't like the captain's direction for the ship, I need to get off that ship. So I did. [Liz recently stopped attending a Korean church.] I don't think a little maintenance work is enough to fix the overall problems within Korean churches." One of the problems Liz experienced was her church's way of perceiving some people, including herself, as "headaches" because leaders did not know which group to direct them toward; for example, Liz did not belong in the young adult group or the married couples group. This conveyed the message to Liz, "Please come back after you get married. You are not welcome yet." All my interviewees shared a similar sense of exclusion or isolation in their church settings, regardless of their ages. Sophie, the youngest interviewee at age 30, also related to this sense of exclusion.

Sharing her frustration regarding sermons that she could hardly relate to as a single woman, Joanna observed, "I know never-married singles are not in the majority. We are like unspecified individuals who remain in preachers' blind spots. We seem like a deserted group." Sadly, Joanna's impressions found support in the experiences described by Kristine, a 31-year-old Ph.D. student. Kristine spoke of a unique situation within the young adult group at her church because of the unexpected influx of a number of people over 35 from one of the megachurches in the same town. Expressing a lot of disappointment in the other church's decision, Kristine said, "I don't know the logistics of how that was done. But that church forced people over 35 out of the young adult group." She continued, "I didn't think that was a good way to really help the people in that age group. What churches are supposed to do is include people and help them grow, not force them out of the group they are comfortable with."

Although I had previously heard about what happened to people over 35 at that megachurch, every time I have revisited Kristine's remarks about what occurred, as well as other interviewees' experiences, through the process of analysis and coding the data, my frustration has grown. Kristine's church situation overlaps with Joanna's words, "a deserted group." Data analysis and the coding process have enabled me to relate to my interviewees' frustrations and disappointments with churches at a deeper level because there appear to be no seats prepared for never-married single people around the table of fellowship in today's Korean churches. It is a shame for Korean churches to have a group of people feeling deserted within them.

What shocked me more than the confirmation of my hypothesis about never-married single women's positions at the margins of churches, however, is that not all my research partners were able to name what they have experienced as wrong. Although I did not ask additional questions to find out more about the reasons for their perceptions, I suspect that internalizing the norm of the marriage and family discourse made them incapable of noticing this unjust method of control. Further, I was surprised by my research partners' willingness to sacrifice themselves in a future relationship. I suspect the urge to sacrifice their selves resulted from socialization within a sexist culture that views women's roles as including being "subservient beings . . . helpmates of men or sex objects" to satisfy men's desires.[9] I find it urgent, then, to construct a theological understanding that will cultivate women's capacities for mutuality with their future partners. (I will introduce my research partners' voices related to this matter later.) Thus, I envision faith communities where never-married single people experience the empowerment to resist cultural expectations, sing their own songs, and live their lives to the fullest.

7.4. Church as an A Cappella Choir

The project titled, *A Cappella: A Report on Realities, Concerns, Expectations and Barriers Experienced by Adolescent Women in Canada* (1990), provides some inspiration as I envision a church where never-married single women are empowered to become authors of their lives, dismantling the involuntary isolation and exclusion that my interviewees underwent in one form or another. Dealing with adolescent girls between the ages of 11 and 19 and their teachers' experiences of being young and female during the 1990s, a

---

9. Fiorenza, *Discipleship of Equals*, 57.

period of gender-role upheaval, the project regards these young women's lives as being like singing *a cappella*.[10] Given that *a cappella* is a genre of music for groups or soloists to perform without instrumental accompaniment, the project indicates how challenging it is for young Canadian women to sing their own rhythms without any instrumental music that supports them. In contrast to *a cantata*, "a vocal composition with an instrumental accompaniment," singing *a cappella* is a riskier business because it is easier for singers to lose their own pitches.[11] When instruments provide singers with a familiar melody, it becomes easier for singers to keep on track.

I think never-married single women in today's Korean churches are also facing the challenge of singing their own rhythms and pitches without any background music to support them and help them keep on track. After my fourth interview, I added the question, "Has there ever been a never-married single woman as a role model around you?" to my questionnaire because I had sensed the importance of significant people's influences on their single status. Although most of my interviewees' parents encouraged them to pursue their dreams, as I indicated above, no one has had a never-married single women as a role model. This can be interpreted as an absence of background melodies to support their ways of being.

To make it worse, there are very loud melodies flowing around them, demanding that they join them under the name of "normality." Referring to violence toward never-married single women in some time periods, Carol Anderson, Susan Stewart, and Sona Dimidjian state in *Flying Solo* (1994) that "single women have faced immense pressure to marry for hundreds of years. . . . single women were viewed as so evil and subversive that they faced not only stigma but overt violence."[12] Today's singles are not convicted of witchcraft and burned at the stake like single women in New England during the 1600s and 1700s were. Many things have gotten better. However, hostility toward and stigmatization of single women remain almost the same, even in church communities.

I think that violence toward never-married single women today has another form: "the violence of assimilation."[13] In her essay, "Engaging Diversity and Difference: From Practices of Exclusion to Practices of Practi-

10. Canadian Teacher's Federation, *A Cappella*.

11. *Wikipedia*, s.v. "Cantata," last modified March 1, 2016, https://web.archive.org/web/*/https://en.wikipedia.org/wiki/Cantata.

12. Anderson, Stewart, and Dimidjian, *Flying Solo*, 51.

13. Gill-Austern, "Engaging Diversity and Difference," 31.

cal Solidarity," Brita Gill-Austern summarizes the four forms of violence related to differences among people identified by Miroslav Volf in *Exclusion and Embrace* (1996): the violence of expulsion, the violence of assimilation, subjugating the other, and exclusion through the indifference of abandonment. Among these four types of practices of exclusion, the violence of assimilation resonates for me more than the others in relation to my interviewees' lived experiences. The violence of assimilation takes a milder form than the violence of expulsion, such as ethnic cleansing, does. Nevertheless, it is still violent because it does not allow the other to be who she really is but rather dictates the way to be.

I think that churches' general attitude toward never-married single people is well conveyed through Liz's remarks summing up the message they send: "Please come back after you get married. You are not welcome yet." This message is an example of a tacit practice of exclusion that can be considered a form of the violence of assimilation. It is not articulated outright, yet it is too obvious to miss. Despite Maxine Denham's assertion that church needs to be "a place where women [can] experience a transformation of cultural expectations rather than pressure to conform to the secular expectation," I think that the marriage and family discourse is so domineering, in churches as well as the general society, that never-married single women easily lose their pitches in the church communities to which they belong.[14] Their communities barely recognize their rhythms.

I envision church as an *a cappella* choir where all pitches are respected and honored as critical components for the whole choir's harmony. To become such choirs, Korean churches need to become counter-communities in terms of resisting the cultural biases that are not true to today's never-married single women's lived experiences, and they need to construct a theological anthropology that promotes the full humanity of never-married single women. Further, I hope Korean churches, as counter-communities, become a source of resistance to the cultural myth of the "good" woman. I believe such resistance is an essential component of empowering never-married single women to live their lives to the fullest and become authors of their own lives. Let us now examine what I mean by "counter-communities."

---

14. Denham, "Life-Styles: A Culture in Transition," 175.

7.5. Counter-Communities as a Source of Resistance

For my vision of counter-communities, I am indebted to *Rooted in Jesus Christ* (2009) by Daniel Izuzquiza. Izuzquiza introduces the works of John Yoder, an influential Anabaptist theologian of the twentieth century. Yoder critiques the Constantinian shift that occurred in the fourth century because of its influence on the church's self-understanding. Yoder's view, as recapitulated by Izuzquiza, is as follows: "Instead of being the social embodiment of a new kind of human relations, the church has considered itself as the soul of the existing society."[15] Challenging the practical alliance between church and state that has dominated Western history, Izuzquiza insists that "Christian communities should incarnate an alternative way of living" through revolutionary nonviolence.[16] In fact, Izuzquiza's vision for churches is not new, in that early churches were themselves counter-communities.

Elizabeth Schüssler Fiorenza's book, *In Memory of Her* (1985), describes well the counter-cultural elements of Jesus' movement. Based on Jesus' counter-cultural value of inclusiveness, Fiorenza argues that it is even "possible for women to become Jesus' disciples."[17] Jesus' call to discipleship was not bound by religion, culture, race, class, or sex. He embodied an alternative world of justice through this call that transcended boundaries and limitations. Identifying Jesus' form of discipleship as a "*discipleship of equals*," Fiorenza challenges today's churches to "proclaim the 'good news' of God's alternative world of justice and love and to make it present by gathering people around the table and inviting everyone without exception to it, by feeding the hungry, healing the sick, and liberating the oppressed."[18] I consider this inclusiveness a foundational value for churches as counter-communities.

Jesus' table fellowship with the poor, sinners, and prostitutes was an excellent example of counter-cultural action. (This topic will be addressed in more detail later in this chapter when I discuss hospitality.) In this vein, Rita Brock and Rebecca Parker's critique of theology that defines virtue as obedience to God makes more sense. Stressing "the virtue of revolt," Brock and Parker assert that "we need a God who delights in revolutionary disobedience and spirited protest. Was not Jesus one such as this—a prophet

---

15. Izuzquiza, *Rooted in Jesus Christ*, 68.
16. Ibid., 69.
17. Fiorenza, "Women in the Early Christian Movement," 88.
18. Fiorenza, *Discipleship of Equals*, 12.

who confronted injustices and risked opposition rather than conform to an empire that enforced its oppressive will through violence?"[19] This kind of revolt is what the term *Protestant* refers to.

I demand that Korean churches take this point seriously when they try to provide care with never-married single women because it is deeply related to generating a deeper transformation of values, worldviews, and attitudes toward never-married single people. I hope contemporary churches will not be places where never-married single people are forced to conform to cultural expectations or be driven away. Given my interviewees' collective experiences of involuntary isolation and exclusion due to the influence of the dominant, culturally-rooted marriage and family discourse, I find recovering the character of counter-communities necessary. Korean churches need to offer counter values to challenge ubiquitously accepted cultural biases about never-married single women, like the ideas that "single women lead lonely, depressing, and incomplete lives," and, "All women are desperate to marry or remarry because marriage is their only real chance for security and happiness."[20] As a first step toward proposing alternative understandings of never-married single women, I would like to invite my research partners to speak one more time.

One of the emergent themes I found in my participants' interviews is their satisfaction with themselves and their lives in general. This provided me with some evidence to argue against the cultural biases toward never-married single women. To the question, "On a scale of zero to ten, how satisfied are you with your life overall and why?" seven of the interviewees answered around 8 or 9. Instead of answering with a number, Kristine responded by saying, "It is different every day. One day I am so thankful for everything. But you know . . . there are days when I don't want to do anything. Luckily, I haven't gone through many ups and downs . . . For me, my relationship with God is a determining factor for my satisfaction with my life." Grace (a 33-year-old employee of a company) and Shannon (a 42-year-old master's degree student) answered with the number 5, which was the lowest satisfaction among my participants with their lives.

When I asked what would raise life satisfaction, Grace answered, "Having a closer job, I guess. I am so tired from the long commute. I have worked at this company for four years. But one year ago I was transferred to my current branch. It has been exhausting to spend hours and hours on the

---

19. Brock and Parker, *Proverbs of Ashes*, 31.
20. Anderson, Stewart, and Dimidjian, *Flying Solo*, 64.

road." She continued, saying, "Maybe a promotion would make it higher." When I asked, "Is that all you need to improve your satisfaction about your life?" she said, "A boyfriend would be a plus." Shannon explained her relatively low life satisfaction as follows:

> If you had asked me the same question when I was in Korea, I would have answered a 9 or an 8 because I was pretty happy with my life back then. But my current situation is pretty hard on me. As a person who just came to America [by the time I interviewed Shannon, she had spent one year here in the United States], I feel very isolated. Although I was single in Korea, I always had a lot of friends around me. You know life in Korea, right? It is difficult here for me to start all over again.

Shannon's 5 is more related to her recently uprooted experience as an international student. Given the drastic change in her location, I interpreted her desire for human connection as a desire for relationship in general, not necessarily limited to an intimate relationship. For the purposes of the current study, I think that an 8 or a 9 for her life satisfaction in Korea needs to be taken into consideration.

I consider the three out of the seven who answered with an 8 or a 9 as about the same as those who answered with a 10 because they are pretty much happy with their lives but are not sure what it would be like to be completely happy, as represented by the number 10. I interpreted their 8's or 9's as more of an expression of humility rather than an expression of a lack of satisfaction. Angelina (a 38-year-old small business owner) stated with a big smile, "I am pretty happy with my life. But I don't want to give the number 10 as an answer because I don't know what true happiness is like." Liz's response was similar to Angelina's. Liz said, "In my opinion, the rest of the 2 perhaps might not be met in this world. How dare I say that I am happy 10 out of 10? But I am pretty happy with my life for sure." Sophie answered with a 9, commenting, "My satisfaction will reach a 10 when sanctification is achieved." Julie and Joanna shared a very similar nuance as they explained their reasons for giving an 8.

Although all of my interviewees acknowledged that marriage would enhance their satisfaction with life in some ways, marriage is not the greatest factor in their happiness and completeness. In light of Ruether's admonition that "whatever diminishes or denies the full humanity of women must be presumed not to reflect the divine or an authentic relation to the divine, or to reflect the authentic nature of things, or to be the message or work of an authentic redeemer or a community of redemption," I view the idea that women can be whole only through marriage as the opposite of redemptive.[21] I hope Korean churches become counter-communities by constructing a theological anthropology that is congruent with today's never-married women's lived experiences and their self understandings. When a more deliberately developed theological anthropology of the female is produced (this is an area in which I think scholars need to invest their energy in the future), never-married single women will experience the feminist theological goal of liberation and transformation. Continuing to construct more holistic theological anthropologies will eventually bring liberation and transformation not only to never-married women but also to married men and women and the whole natural world, from which patriarchic theologies have alienated humans.

Further, as counter-communities, I encourage Korean churches to propose an alternative theological foundation for the image of "good" women as a means to empower never-married single women. Anderson, Stewart, and Dimidjian capture well this dominant image of "good" women through the timeless, perhaps universal, childhood heroine, Cinderella. They quote the opening lines of Walt Disney's film version of this story: "Cinderella was abused, humiliated, and finally forced to become a servant in her own house. *And yet, through it all, Cinderella remained ever gentle and kind.*"[22] The need to challenge this image of "good" women emerged from my data analysis process.

There is no particular question that allowed me to obtain a view about "good" women from my research partners. However, the term "good woman" was one of the recurring key words from a number of analyses. Grace said, "Even if both a husband and a wife work, women ought to sacrifice more, right? I would consider quitting my job if my husband wanted me to." Speaking of her expectations about marriage, Kristine stated,

> " . . . well, I think my concert would end with marriage instead of starting with marriage. . . . Nowadays it is true that a husband and a wife share domestic chores. But still there are things only a mom can do for her children. If I become a mother and a wife, that means I need to sacrifice my life for them. That's why I think that my concert will be over with marriage."

---

21. Ruether, *Sexism and God-Talk*, 19.
22. Anderson, et al., *Flying Solo*, 57.

With some differences in degree, Angelina and Kathy also expressed a willingness to sacrifice themselves in a marriage.

I do not perceive this willingness as something bad. I was actually impressed by their generous attitudes of being prepared to give up their selves for their marriages. This also contradicts a cultural bias about never-married single women being immature and opinionated. However, I am concerned that their sense of moral responsibility—to give up their selves for marriage—is rooted in a cultural understanding of "good" women as women who put others' needs first. Moreover, the theological understanding that relates selfishness to sin reinforces this already inculcated image of a "good" woman. I also sense a possible exploitation of women within families in that these professional women will be expected to play the role of superwomen, being responsible for domestic chores while they have full-time jobs, all in pursuit of the "virtue of sacrifice."

Feminist theologians have developed fresh understandings about selfishness and self-love since Valerie Saiving's work, "The Human Situation: A Feminine View" (1979). In this essay, Saiving argued for the necessity of redefining traditional theological understandings of sin and redemption using feminine experiences. Since male-based theologies identified sin with self-assertion and love with selflessness, Saiving assessed these understandings of sin and love as not necessarily applicable to female experiences or helpful to females. It is through too much self-giving or selflessness that many a woman suffers to the point that "she gives too much of herself, so that nothing remains of her own uniqueness; she can become merely an emptiness, almost a zero, without value to herself, to her fellow men, or, perhaps, even to God."[23] For women, underdevelopment or negation of the self is often their sin. Churches, as counter-communities, need to teach never-married single women to develop self-love rather than selflessness and self-assertion rather than self-negation for their spiritual growth.

Lastly, churches, as counter-communities, need to embody alternative power dynamics through decentralized communities based on shared power. I envision church as a place where all people relate to one another, not in a hierarchical manner of domination and control, but in an equal fashion as kin, with respect and love. This is the reason why I employ the word *kin-dom* in lieu of *kingdom*. Since Isasi-Diaz's critique of the common term, *kingdom*, feminist scholars have replaced *kingdom* with the term

---

23. Saiving, "The Human Situation," 37.

kin-dom. I consider this movement very promising because our language matters; it influences our modes of being in profound ways.

Isasi-Diaz rejected the word *kingdom* because of the sexist, hierarchical, and elitist connotations of the term. On the contrary, for her, the word *kin-dom* makes it clear that "when the fullness of God becomes a day-to-day reality in the world at large, we will all be sisters and brothers—kin to each other; we will indeed be the family of God."[24] As I explain in Chapter 6 about the power of metaphors, church as the kin-dom of God represents a counter-community where equality and mutuality override hierarchy and domination. The traditional understanding of power as "power-over" needs to be changed to a notion of "power-with" or "power-for."

According to Sheryl Kujawa-Holbrook, "One of the reasons why so many attempts at pastoral care fail to bring authentic healing and reconciliation is that the overall dominant culture within American society often does not recognize or strive to correct the deep power imbalances experienced by all marginalized people."[25] I do not think that Kujawa-Holbrook's claim is true only within American society in general. In my view, church communities also lack efforts to amend power imbalances experienced by people at the margins. Given the clerical structures that continue to reinforce structures of hierarchy and domination, the effort to resolve the issue of power imbalances within church communities is necessary. The need to distribute power equally is particularly important for never-married single women because of the long period of denial of their power and agency. Harmonizing melodies are possible when intentional support is given to help weaker parts be heard.

Ministers need to remember that church communities are not exempt from the politics of gender, race, class, and so on associated with hierarchies of knowledge and social marginalization.[26] Politics are deeply enmeshed everywhere, even in church communities. However, some ministers are not aware of how much power they have in relation to their congregants. Others are aware, but misuse their position in order to maintain their existing power and the status quo. Nancy Ramsay asserts that "power is most likely to be misused when it is denied."[27] A denial of power does not make a church community exempt from power dynamics. When ministers

---

24. Isasi-Díaz, "Solidarity: Love of Neighbor in the 21st Century," 306.
25. Kujawa-Holbrook, "Love and Power," 13.
26. White, *Narrative Practice*, 49–50.
27. Ramsay, *Pastoral Diagnosis*, 113.

care for never-married single women, they need to use their power within the framework of shared power, power-with or power-for, instead of power-over.

Larry Graham upholds the significance of attention to power dynamics for practices of care. Remarking about the destructiveness of imbalanced power, he warns that "unless such a hegemony is challenged and modified by more positive configurations, great evil can occur."[28] Acknowledging the power imbalance between ministers and laypeople, ministers need to invite congregants to a place where they can access the power to speak by sharing their stories. This can be accomplished through an intentional type of small group where people can tell their stories. Further, I want to boldly suggest that Korean churches come up with alternative ways to share the pulpit with congregants because the notion of shared power is hardly obtained within the current worship service style. When people are exposed to more stories, more possibilities for tearing down the hegemonic domination of one way of living are created. Further, I think this can be one way toward more positive configurations of power in that to be able to speak is a means to obtain power.

Graham's description of victimizing and chaotic power supports the idea of striving for decentralized communities based on mutuality:

> Victimizing and chaotic power exists when either one person or group is coerced into becoming the receptor of the influence of others quite apart from their own desires, needs, and aspirations. It also exists when there is such a power vacuum that legitimate desires, needs, and aspirations of individuals or groups of individuals have no viable means of validation or fulfillment.[29]

According to Graham, victimizing power robs individuals and groups of genuine agential power. To bring healing to those who are victimized, Graham proposes a mode of shared power "which is expressed in reciprocal agency and receptivity in a respectful covenantal framework."[30] Given the oppressive situation under which never-married single women live, as articulated in Chapter 5, I demand that Korean churches pay attention to imbalanced power and its operating forces upon those who are excluded from the table of fellowship.

---

28. Graham, *Care of Persons, Care of Worlds*, 138.
29. Ibid., 140.
30. Ibid.

7.6. The Notions of Divine Hospitality and Alterity

I find the notion of divine hospitality as incarnated by Jesus and the notion of alterity helpful in that these two notions are germane to bringing counter-communities into reality. These two notions have potentials to enhance Korean churches' capability to become a choir with many parts embracing voices from the margin. Further, the violence assimilation will stop as people embody attitudes understanding these two notion, Specifically, when I think about never-married single women whose lives are like they are singing their own rhythms without any background support, the concept of radical hospitality becomes even more critical. (The difference between "hospitality" and "radical hospitality" will be explained later.) These women's lives remind me of "the condition of irreducible pluralism" that John Caputo names as a postmodern condition (employing Lyotard's term).[31] People today need to come to terms with the multiplicity of lifestyles and ways of being that exist. It is this condition of irreducible pluralism that contemporary churches are facing and need to respond to. To understand radical hospitality and alterity is one of the priorities that Christian churches must endeavor to incarnate in this postmodern age. So, what do I mean by Jesus' radical hospitality and alterity?

7.6.1. Divine Hospitality

At the beginning of this research project, I referred to Jesus' derogatory nickname—"friend of tax collectors and sinners"—to point out Jesus' radical practices of hospitality, and I wondered about ways in which to restore them in today's churches. Reflecting on my research partners' experiences of isolation and exclusion because of the prevalent yet unrecognized violence of assimilation in today's churches, the thirst for radical hospitality became even bigger. As I envision churches as counter-communities where diverse and multiple ways of being are acknowledged and encouraged, I am even more attracted to this concept because how people relate to others plays an important role in such communities. Hence, I want to more closely examine radical hospitality as it is described in the Bible. The parables of banquets in the gospels of Mathew (the wedding banquet) and Luke (the great banquet) well demonstrate what divine hospitality looks like.[32] When

---

31. Caputo, *What Would Jesus Deconstruct?*, 42.
32. Matthew 22:1–14 and Luke 14:15–24.

the invited refuse to come, the enraged host asks his servants to "go out quickly into the streets and alleys of the town and bring in the poor, the crippled, and the lame" (Lk 14:21). Can you imagine a banquet hall filled with the poor, the crippled, and the lame?

According to Caputo, radical hospitality in these parables means "welcoming the unwelcomed and receiving the uninvited."[33] Everyone can welcome the welcomed and receive the invited. This is what hospitality is about. However, *radical hospitality* requires us to go beyond our understanding and reason. The meaning of *radical hospitality* becomes more comprehensible as Caputo contrasts hospitality in the world with hospitality in the realm of the kingdom of God:

> In the world, hospitality is constituted by a cozy circle of insiders, by the rules of the club, where all sorts of folks who are different need not apply. In the world, hospitality is a strong force—*hostis + potens*, having the power of the master of the house over the guest—in which one fortifies oneself against the unwelcome intrusion of the other. But in the kingdom, hospitality is a weak force that leaves itself entirely unfortified.[34]

In the world, the concept of hospitality is oddly built upon a great deal of inhospitality. This is what Parker Palmer means when he observes, "an intimate community is formed by an act of exclusion—'we' are in and 'they' are out."[35] There is a clear demarcation between the invited and the uninvited. Being invited is a signpost designating the privilege of being an insider. This mindset seems to have lain behind the actions of Michaele and Tareq Salahi, a married couple from Virginia, when they attended a White House state dinner in 2009 as uninvited guests.[36] The Salahis entered the state dinner for the Indian Prime minister, Manmohan Singh, as uninvited guests. The Salahis were caught because they posted photos of themselves posing with Vice President Joe Biden and Chief of Staff Rahm Emanuel on Facebook to indicate their up-close access to some of Washington's elite. The Salahis wanted to show they were *in* the club.

---

33. Caputo, *What Would Jesus Deconstruct?*, 77.
34. Caputo, *The Weakness of God*, 262.
35. Palmer, *The Company of Strangers*, 130.
36. Wikipedia, s.v. "2009 U. S. State Dinner Security Breaches," last modified March 16, 2016, https://web.archive.org/web/*/https://en.wikipedia.org/wiki/2009_U.S._state_dinner_security_breaches.

The hospitality that these parables of the banquet depict is utterly different. God asks us to go beyond our typical ways of thinking by expanding our hospitality even to our enemies. Calling this kind of radical hospitality "sheer madness," Caputo identifies God's way of ruling in the kin-dom of God with "the rule of hospitality" that "takes the form of the alogic of welcoming the other."[37] Jesus incarnated God's radical approach of welcoming others throughout his ministry by inviting people at the margins into the center of his relational circle. Stressing the inclusiveness of Jesus' call to his disciples, Fiorenza asserts, "The gospels affirm in various ways that Jesus' call to discipleship had precedence over all other obligations, religious duties, and family ties."[38] I think today's churches are called to incarnate God's radical hospitality here on earth by breaking down the fortified walls of norms and regulations that marginalize those who fall outside of them. The notion of hospitality will enable today's church to recover its core character of inclusiveness of all people. In light of God's way of welcoming others, today's churches need to rethink the manners in which they relate to a plurality of voices and choices, races, cultures, and religions.

Henri Nouwen sheds light on a way to implement this notion of divine hospitality in our current context. He indicates that the critical role of hospitality is to create a "free and fearless space where brotherhood and sisterhood can be formed and fully experienced."[39] This fearless space is generated when a hostess does not require a stranger to change in any way when she invites the stranger to her house. Thus, Nouwen understands hospitality to be about creating emptiness filled with friendship. Within this friendly emptiness, guests feel free to become who they really are, rather than being forced to conform to the norms of the hosts. Nouwen remarks,

> The paradox of hospitality is that it wants to create emptiness, not a fearful emptiness, but a friendly emptiness where strangers can enter and discover themselves as created free; free to sing their own songs, speak their own languages, dance their own dances; free also to leave and follow their own vocations. Hospitality is not a subtle invitation to adopt the life style of the host, but the gift of a chance for the guest to find his own.[40]

---

37. Caputo, *The Weakness of God*, 262.
38. Fiorenza, *Discipleship of Equals*, 42.
39. Nouwen, *Reaching Out*, 66.
40. Ibid., 72.

As I reflect on the idea of a space of friendly emptiness, I feel deep gratitude for the friendly emptiness offered to me by a number of American people: professors, clients, and church members. They are those who have tried to call me by my first name, "Hyoju," which must be unfamiliar to them. After being called "JuLee" for the two years of my hospital CPE training because of the difficulty Americans have with pronouncing the syllable "Hyo," I realized how much I like my Korean first name, *Hyoju*. When I moved to California, I decided to go by my Korean first name. Sometimes, when I introduce myself using my foreign first name, some people casually and suggestively ask, "Why don't you have an American name?" Although I do not necessarily feel inhospitality from these comments, Nouwen's remarks allow me to realize how hospitable an action it is to call someone by her first name, regardless of the challenges in pronouncing it.

Those who have endeavored to pronounce my name and call me by it have enabled me to sing my own songs, allowing me a space where I can find who God is, who I am, and who my neighbors are in my own way in this foreign country. Just as a hostess does not require a change when she invites a stranger to her house, the hosts of the banquets in the Gospels do not ask the unwelcomed to change. When today's churches embody Caputo's and Nouwen's understandings of hospitality, they will function as counter-communities where various, multiple ways of harmoniously and respectfully co-existing with one another, without domesticating anyone's way of being, are lived out. Further, the practice of hospitality will make churches communities to which all people are invited, without exception, bringing an end to the violence of assimilation.

7.6.2. Understanding Alterity

A church as an *a cappella* choir needs to be a place where all lifestyles are validated, welcomed, and encouraged, thus resisting the hegemonic acceptance of only one way of living. Given that the essence of colonization is to impose the language, customs, and ways of life of one group on all, the domination of the marriage and family discourse can be interpreted as hegemonic colonialization.[41] In agreement with Emmanuel Lartey's postcolonial reading of the Tower of Babel story in Genesis 11:1–9, I consider God's act of "confusing" (*babel*) the languages of the whole world (v. 7) a divine action of advocating diversity instead of the hegemonic power of

---

41. Lartey, *Postcolonializing God*, 3.

one language. God acted in order to save the endangered diversity of all creation by confusing people's languages. I do not think God's desire for diversity is limited to the dimension of language. Rather, God continues to prefer diversity to hegemonic denomination.

I think church as an *a cappella* choir become tangible when today's churches respond to the call to incarnate God's desire to dispel and diffuse any type of hegemony. To respond to this call, "A stronger notion of 'alterity' (otherness) and its implications" could serve as a solid foundation for church communities that hope to extend their welcome to others without domesticating their voices."[42] By using the term *alterity*, Jacques Derrida stresses the otherness of humans as being like the way in which God is wholly other to us. Derrida's phrase, "*tout autre est tout autre*," which can be translated, "every other is totally other," names a critical aspect of this concept.[43] Derrida regards the ultimate concern of both ethics and religion as making no distinction between "the infinite alterity of God and that of every human."[44] When today's churches value Derrida's notion of alterity at the heart of their beings, never-married single women will be able to keep singing their melodies, enriching the harmony of the whole community.

Elaine Graham asserts, "Any community which attempts to adopt a totalizing claim to knowledge and truth would therefore be denying the fundamental condition of alterity by destroying the 'Others' of non-meaning, provisionality or occluded groups and perspectives."[45] If churches do not know how to embrace others, instead requiring conformity to their clear ideas of what life is all about, the alterity of others begins to crumble. This violates Jesus' command to his followers to "love your neighbor as yourself."[46] Any church that hopes to participate in God's redemptive activities in today's pluralistic world needs to know how to relate to others without domesticating their unique voices. I find that the concept of alterity fits well with Nouwen's idea of hospitality as providing a space of "friendly emptiness."

Bons-Storm's concept of "theology as a choir of many voices" provides a foundation for embodying a friendly emptiness that honors people's

---

42. Graham, *Transforming Practice*, 8.
43. Derrida, *The Gift of Death and Literature in Secret*, 82.
44. Ibid., 84.
45. Graham, *Transforming Practice*, 168.
46. Mark 12:31.

alterity.[47] For me, Bons-Storm's view acknowledges both the limitations of human beings and a deep appreciation for each individual. Thus, she affirms the presence of God within every human being, making each person worthy of participating in the process of constructing theology. Diverse aspects of God that cannot be contained in a small box have been revealed as the monotone melody of white males' theologies have been enriched by various pitches and sounds from various groups' understandings of God. Given that many different voices have expanded the monotonous, confining rhythm of the theological enterprise dominated by white males for almost two hundred years, different voices need to be welcomed. More people's lived experiences need to be validated to the point that theologies modify themselves along the way. Herein lies a reason for churches to cultivate radical hospitality through paying attention to never-married women's rhythms, which are perhaps unfamiliar to long-time singers (the married majority), in order to renovate their own theologies.

When diverse stories are valued, multiple ways for faithful living will emerge. Without domesticating anyone's voice, no matter how faint or foreign it might sound, church must be a place where never-married single women are empowered to retrieve the right to tell their truths in their own languages. The meaning of the gospel as expounded by Joel McClure, a minister at Water's Edge in Hudsonville, Michigan, makes the pathways to being a church clearer. According to McClure,

> The gospel is not that we agree with some abstract proposition in order to qualify to go to heaven when we die but an invitation to live in a new way of life. Sharing the good news is not only about conversation. It is about inviting someone to walk with you relationally. . . . It is an invitation to participate in God's redemptive activities.[48]

Today's churches are called to incarnate God's redemptive activities for all people by walking with them relationally. It is not a hierarchical approach but a relational and egalitarian one. All need to treat each other with the same tantamount reverence they have for God as the wholly other. As all members of a church walk together and invite others, providing them with a friendly emptiness that honors their alterity, more people will be able to experience kin-dom in our midst.

---

47. Bons-Storm, *The Incredible Woman*, 126.
48. Gibbs and Bolger, *Emerging Churches*, 56.

7.7. Conclusion

In this chapter, I tried to answer the questions, "What ought to happen?" and "How do churches go about making it happen?" in the face of the involuntary exclusion and isolation of never-married single women. Identifying four key tasks of practical theology, Richard Osmer views the normative and pragmatic tasks as being central to practical theology as an academic discipline.[49] For a particular phenomenon, practical theology tries to answer the questions, "What is happening?" (the descriptive-empirical task) and "Why is it happening?" (the interpretive task). These efforts become meaningful only when followed with responses to the questions, "What ought to happen?" (the normative task) and "How might we respond?" (the pragmatic task). It is never enough just to know the phenomenon as it is and understand the reasons for it. Practical theology must take the further step "to enable faithful living and authentic Christian practice."[50] As I stated in Chapter 4, whereas the starting point of practical theology is human lived experiences, the ending point of it is to encourage and enable faithful practices in cultivating the kin-dom in our midst.

All Christian theologies share the call to the normative and pragmatic tasks to the extent that Christians pray for the coming of God's kin-dom and the fulfillment of God's will on earth as it is in heaven. This is the reason why McFague demands that all theologians and students of religion respond to the call to deconstruct and reconstruct the traditional symbols of Christian faith, moving beyond the task of hermeneutics. McFague argues, "Christian theology, in our time at least, cannot be merely or mainly hermeneutics, that is, interpretation of the tradition, a translation of ancient creeds and concepts to make them relevant for contemporary culture."[51] What is as important as the task of interpretation for today's theologies, according to McFague, is to engender changes in our time. To do so, "theology must be self-consciously constructive, willing to think differently than in the past."[52] In my estimation, McFague's endeavor to construct alternative images of God as mother, lover, and friend is commensurate with the normative and pragmatic tasks of practical theology because it intends to bring changes for more faithful living.

---

49. Osmer, *Practical Theology*, 11.
50. Swinton and Mowat, *Practical Theology and Qualitative Research*, 9.
51. McFague, *Models of God*, 21.
52. Ibid.

A VISION FOR CHURCHES

I offer a metaphor of church as an *a cappella* choir where all members are respected and valued as indispensable elements for creating harmonious music. To become such choirs, churches have to function as counter-communities that can be sources of resistance through supporting and empowering individuals to become authors of their own lives by using narrative pastoral practices that encourage people to keep reconstructing their stories and identities from different perspectives. The notion of divine hospitality as incarnated in Jesus' ministry of table fellowship challenges contemporary churches' practices of exclusion and the violence of assimilation. Understanding God's preference for diversity over hegemonic domination, Korean churches need to cultivate the openness to embrace others by acknowledging their alterity.

Thus, Korean churches need to offer counter values not only to challenge ubiquitously accepted cultural biases about never-married single women but also to promote the full humanity of never-married single women. God calls women to more than looking "pretty" and serving their families. Never-married single women must come of age with an understanding of themselves as human beings with autonomy, people who are partners with others, and Jesus' disciples. Churches that endeavor to empower never-married single women to flourish will construct alternative theological foundations for theological anthropology and the concept of "good" women. These efforts will benefit not only never-married women but also their families and larger communities. It is my hope that such transformations in churches and communities will extend not only to the whole human race but also to the ecological world.

An alternative world of justice and love for all people is not meant to come only through the participation of half of the human race. When more women participate in the decision-making process at the table of fellowship, social structures centered around men will be transformed. Likewise, one-sided, married-centered structures of churches and society need to be transformed through giving more single women access to speak with authority. Although I propose my vision as tentative and provisional, when people understand and live out this vision seriously, I believe it has the potential to embrace people at the margins so they can participate in the decision-making processes at the table of fellowship. Eventually, as more and more people are included, a better world will be created for all people.

Appendix A

Email to send to my acquaintances

Hi,

I'm a Ph.D. student in practical theology with an emphasis on spiritually integrative care and counseling at Claremont School of Theology in Claremont, California. For my dissertation, I am seeking to do research in order to develop a postmodern pastoral care and counseling strategy for marginalized, never-married single women. I find never-married single women to be on the margins of the margins in the average Korean local church, and I observe an ever-increasing need "for the church to formulate a theology around singles, one that affirms and celebrates single people, one that welcomes them into the Christian life and the life of the church" (Debrah Farrington, *One Like Jesus: Converstions on the Single Life*). My research has three aims: (1) to learn about the lived experiences of Protestant Korean-American never-married single women over thirty with a minimum of a college education as a way to lift up their knowledge as opposed to the domineering grand narratives of marriage and family; (2) to place these voices in conversation with existing literature and circulated stereotypes; and (3) to envision an ecclesiology where God's justice and Jesus' radical hospitality are embodied.

My starting point is to listen to the voices of never-married single women regarding their own lived experiences. While there has been some research done on white, middle-class, professional single women, we know almost nothing about the lifestyles and personal values of Korean-American never-married single women and how they experience the traditional teachings of the church about marriage and family. Thus, I would like to invite you to participate in a one-hour, semi-structured interview with me. Questions that I would ask you to answer are the following:

- "Please share with me the ways in which church teachings about marriage and family affect you."
- "On a scale of zero to ten, how satisfied are you with your life overall and why?"
- "Have you felt excluded in your church community? If yes, please share specific occasions when you felt excluded."
- "What is the most recent sermon you heard that instilled a sense of hope in you?"
- "What are your sources of life fulfilment?"
- "What is your joy?"
- "What is your hope for your church congregation?"

Dr. Duane Bidwell is the chairperson of my dissertation committee. To respond or to ask questions, please email me at hyoju.lee@cst.edu or call me at (973) 713-3009.

Thank you for taking the time to read this and respond.

Warm regards,

Hyoju

Appendix B

Email to send out to churches in the Los Angeles area

Dear congregational leader:

I'm a Ph.D. student in practical theology with an emphasis on spiritually integrative care and counseling at Claremont School of Theology in Claremont, California. For my dissertation, I am seeking to do research in order to develop a postmodern pastoral care and counseling strategy for marginalized, never-married single women. I find never-married single women to be on the margins of the margins in the average Korean local church, and I observe an ever-increasing need "for the church to formulate a theology around singles, one that affirms and celebrates single people, one that welcomes them into the Christian life and the life of the church" (Debrah Farrington, *One Like Jesus: Conversations on the Single Life*). My research has three aims: (1) to learn about the lived experiences of Protestant Korean-American never-married single women over thirty with a minimum of a college education as a way to lift up their knowledge as opposed to the domineering grand narratives of marriage and family; (2) to place these voices in conversation with existing literature and circulated stereotypes; and (3) to envision an ecclesiology where God's justice and Jesus' radical hospitality are embodied.

My starting point is to listen to the voices of never-married single women regarding their own lived experiences. While there has been some research done on white, middle-class, professional single women, we know almost nothing about the lifestyles and personal values of Korean-American never-married single women and how they experience the traditional

EMAIL TO SEND OUT TO CHURCHES IN THE LOS ANGELES AREA

teachings of the church about marriage and family. Thus, I would like to ask you to make an announcement that I am recruiting Protestant Korean-American never-married single women over thirty who have a college education to participate in my study. Research participants would be interviewed by me in a one-hour, semi-structured interview. When you announce this study, please let your congregants know that they have a choice and their participation is entirely voluntary. Questions that I will be asking participants are as follows:

- "Please share with me the ways in which church teachings about marriage and family affect you."
- "On a scale of zero to ten, how satisfied are you with your life overall and why?"
- "Have you felt excluded in your church community? If yes, please share specific occasions when you felt excluded."
- "What is the most recent sermon you heard that instilled a sense of hope in you?"
- "What are your sources of life fulfilment?"
- "What is your joy?"
- "What is your hope for your church congregation?"

Dr. Duane Bidwell is the chairperson of my dissertation committee. To respond or to ask questions, interested persons can email me at hyoju.lee@cst.edu or call me at (973) 713-3009.

Thank you for taking the time to read this and respond.

Warm regards,

Hyoju

Appendix C

Interview Consent Form

You are invited to participate in a research study entitled, "Redeeming Singleness: Postmodern Pastoral Care and Counseling for Marginalized, Never-Married Single Women." This research is being conducted under the supervision of Dr. Duane Bidwell of Claremont School of Theology, 1325 N. College Ave., Claremont, CA 91711, dbidwell@cst.edu, (909) 447–2528.

The purpose of this research study is to explore pastoral care and counseling strategies for the marginalized in our postmodern world by examining Protestant Korean-American never-married single women's lived experiences of church teachings that stress family and marriage. Your participation in the study will contribute to a better understanding of the lived experiences of Korean-American never-married single women so as to engender faithful transformations in churches toward embodying God's justice and Jesus' radical hospitality. You are free to contact the investigator using the information below to discuss the study.
Hyoju Lee, 1325 N. College Ave., D123, Claremont, CA 91711, 973–713–3009, hyoju.lee@cst.edu
You must be at least 18 years old to participate.

If you agree to participate:

- The interview will take approximately 60 minutes. Only one interview session is necessary, unless there is a request for a follow-up interview.
- The intent of your participation is to share your lived experiences as a never-married single woman at church as well as in the larger society. I will also ask you to share the sources of your life fulfillment, joys, dreams, and hopes for the church.

INTERVIEW CONSENT FORM

- Your participation will consist in answering the following questions:
    - "Please share with me the ways in which church teachings about marriage and family affect you."
    - "On a scale of zero to ten, how satisfied are you with your life overall and why?"
    - "Have you felt excluded in your church community? If yes, please share specific occasions when you felt excluded."
    - "What is the most recent sermon you heard that instilled a sense of hope in you?"
    - "What are your sources of life fulfilment?"
    - "What is your joy?"
    - "What is your hope for your church congregation?"
- You will not be compensated.

The purpose of this study is to gain insight into practical theology, pastoral care, and/or spiritual care. Participation in this study should not be regarded as—or substituted for—therapy by a licensed professional.

Risks/Benefits/Confidentiality of Data

There is no known risk. However, some of the questions could lead you to feel uncomfortable, embarrassed, sad, tired, etc. There will be no costs for participating. Your name, email address, and other personally identifiable information will be kept confidential during the data collection phase. No personally identifiable information will be publicly released. Your personal information, if collected, will be used solely for tracking purposes. Only my dissertation committee and I will have access to the data during data collection. My dissertation committee consists of Dr. Duane Bidwell, Dr. Rosemary Radford Ruether, and Dr. K. Samuel Lee. When the results of the research are published or discussed in conferences, no information will be included that would reveal your identity. If photographs, videos, or audio recordings of your participation are used for educational purposes, your identity will be protected or disguised. Your information will be stored until February 2016 and then destroyed.

INTERVIEW CONSENT FORM

Participation or Withdrawal

Your participation in this study is voluntary. You may decline to answer any questions and you have the right to withdraw from participation at any time. Withdrawal will not affect your relationship with Claremont School of Theology in any way. If you do not want to continue participating, you may simply stop.

Contacts

If you have any questions about this study or need to update your email address, please contact the primary investigator, Hyoju Lee, at 973-713-3009 or hyoju.lee@cst.edu. This study has been reviewed by the Claremont School of Theology Institutional Review Board and the study number is 29.

Questions about your rights as a research participant.

If you have questions about your rights or are dissatisfied at any time with any part of this study, you can contact, anonymously if you wish, the chair of the Institutional Review Board by phone at (909) 447-6344 or email at irb@cst.edu.

Thank you.

INTERVIEW CONSENT FORM

❁ SIGNATURE OF RESEARCH PARTICIPANT

I have read the information provided above. I have been given an opportunity to ask questions and all of my questions have been answered to my satisfaction. I have been given a copy of this form.

_____

Name of Participant (Please Print)

_____   _____

Signature of Participant   *Date*

_____

Address

_____   _____

Phone   *Email*

◆ SIGNATURE OF WITNESS

My signature as witness certifies that the participant signed this consent form in my presence as his/her voluntary act and deed.

_____

Name of Witness

_____   _____

Signature of Witness   *Date (same as participant's)*

◆ SIGNATURE OF INVESTIGATOR

_____   _____

Signature of Investigator   *Date (same as participant's)*

A copy of this document will be supplied for your records.

Appendix D

Emergent Themes with Master Codes

Emergent Themes	Master Codes
A Sense of Exclusion	God's will
	Lack of people in same age group
	Communal gaze
	Feeling of failure
	Family-oriented church programs
	Headache/Outsider
	Isolation
	Alienation
	Exclusion
The Importance of Community	Social pressures
	A sense of being left behind
	Absence of role models
	Emotional support from immediate family members
	Supportive parents
	Realization of reality of marriage
Overall Satisfaction with Life	Freedom to do whatever they want to do with their lives
	Second career
	Things to learn
	Places to travel
	Financial security
	Health
Good Women	Openness to having husbands and children
	Helpmate
	Desire to give
	Selflessness
	Vicarious satisfaction
A Desire for Partnership and Offspring	Desire to be a mother
	Physiological urgency
	Desire to be settled

Bibliography

Adams, Margaret. *Single Blessedness: Observations on the Single Status in Married Society*. New York: Basic Books, 1976.
Anderson, Carol M., Susan Stewart, and Sona Dimidjian. *Flying Solo: Single Women in Midlife*. New York: W.W. Norton, 1994.
Anderson, Herbert and Freda A. Gardner. *Living Alone*. Louisville: Westminster John Knox, 1997.
Baker, Luther G. "The Personal and Social Adjustment of the Never-Married Woman," *Journal of Marriage and the Family* 30, no. 3 (August 1968): 473–79.
Beels, C. Christian. *A Different Story: The Rise of Narrative in Psychotherapy*. Phoenix: Zeig, Tucker & Theisen, 2001.
Bequaert, Lucia H. *Single Women, Alone and Together*. Boston: Beacon, 1976.
Berquist, Jon L. *Controlling Corporeality: The Body and the Household in Ancient Israel*. New Brunswick: Rutgers University Press, 2002.
Bidwell, Duane R. *Empowering Couples: A Narrative Approach to Spiritual Care*. Creative Pastoral Care and Counseling Series. Minneapolis, MN: Fortress, 2013.
Bons-Storm, Riet. *The Incredible Woman: Listening to Women's Silences in Pastoral Care and Counseling*. Nashville: Abingdon, 1996.
Brock, Rita Nakashima, and Rebecca Ann Parker. *Proverbs of Ashes: Violence, Redemptive Suffering, and the Search for What Saves Us*. Boston: Beacon, 2001.
Bruner, Edward M. "Ethnography as Narrative." In *The Anthropology of Experience*, edited by Victor W. Turner and Edward M. Bruner, 139–55. Urbana: University of Illinois Press, 1986.
Bruner, Jerome S. *Actual Minds, Possible Worlds*. Cambridge, MA.: Harvard University Press, 1986.
Canadian Teacher's Federation. *A Cappella: A Report on the Realities, Concerns, Expectations and Barriers Experienced by Adolescent Women in Canada*. Ottawa, Ontario: Canadian Teachers' Federation, 1990.
Caputo, John D. *The Weakness of God: A Theology of the Event*. Bloomington: Indiana University Press, 2006.
———. *What Would Jesus Deconstruct?: The Good News of Postmodernism for the Church*. Grand Rapids, MI.: Baker Academic, 2007.

BIBLIOGRAPHY

Cavaliere, Victoria. "Seattle Lawmakers Vote to Change Name of Columbus Day Holiday," October 6, 2014. https://web.archive.org/web/*/http://www.reuters.com/article/2014/10/06/us-usa-washington-columbus-idUSKCN0HV27E20141006?feedType=RSS&feedName=domesticNews.

Charmaz, Kathy. *Constructing Grounded Theory*. 2nd ed. London: Sage, 2014.

Chinula, Donald M. "The Tasks of Oppression-Sensitive Pastoral Caregiving and Counseling." In *Injustice and the Care of Souls: Taking Oppression Seriously in Pastoral Care*, edited by Sheryl A. Kujawa-Holbrook and Karen Brown Montagno, 133–38. Minneapolis: Fortress, 2009.

Chopp, Rebecca S. *Saving Work: Feminist Practices of Theological Education*. Louisville, KY.: Westminster John Knox, 1995.

Christ, Carol P. *Rebirth of the Goddess: Finding Meaning in Feminist Spirituality*. Reading, MA.: Addison-Wesley, 1997.

Clark, Elizabeth A., and Herbert Warren Richardson, eds. *Women and Religion: The Original Sourcebook of Women in Christian Thought*. new revised and expanded ed. San Francisco: HarperSanFrancisco, 1996.

Clifford, James. "Introduction: Partial Truth." In *Writing Culture: The Poetics and Politics of Ethnography*, 1–26. Berkeley: University of California Press, 1986.

Clinebell, Howard. "Toward Envisioning the Future of Pastoral Counselingand AAPC." *The Journal of Pastoral Care* 37, no. 3 (September 1983): 180–94.

Coates, Ta-Nehisi. *Between the World and Me*. New York: Spiegel & Grau, 2015.

Combs, Gene, and Jill Freedman. *Symbol, Story, and Ceremony: Using Metaphor in Individual and Family Therapy*. New York: Norton, 1990.

Cone, James H. *God of the Oppressed*. Maryknoll, NY: Orbis, 1975.

Coontz, Stephanie. *Marriage, a History: How Love Conquered Marriage*. New York: Penguin, 2005.

———. *The Social Origins of Private Life: A History of American Families, 1600–1900*. London; New York: Verso, 1988.

———. *The Way We Never Were: American Families and the Nostalgia Trap*. New York: Basic, 1992.

Cooper-White, Pamela. *Shared Wisdom: Use of the Self in Pastoral Care and Counseling*. Minneapolis: Fortress, 2004.

Corbin, Juliet M., and Anselm L. Strauss. *Basics of Qualitative Research: Techniques and Procedures for Developing Grounded Theory*. 3rd ed. Los Angeles: Sage, 2008.

Coyle, Suzanne M. *Re-Storying Your Faith*. Washington: Circle Books, 2013.

Damasio, Antonio R. *The Feeling of What Happens: Body and Emotion in the Making of Consciousness*. New York: Harcourt, 2000.

Dell, Mary Lynn. "Will My Time Ever Come? On Being Single." In *In Her Own Time: Women and Developmental Issues in Pastoral Care*, edited by Jeanne Stevenson-Moessner. Minneapolis: Fortress, 2000.

Denborough, David. *Retelling the Stories of Our Lives: Everyday Narrative Therapy to Draw Inspiration and Transform Experience*. New York: W.W. Norton, 2014.

Denham, Maxine. "Life-Styles: A Culture in Transition." In *Women in Travail and Transition: A New Pastoral Care*, edited by Maxine Glaz and Jeanne Stevenson Moessner, 162–83. Minneapolis: Fortress, 1991.

Denney, Steven. "South Korea's History Textbook Controversy." *The Diplomat*, April 4, 2015. Steven Denney, "South Korea's History Textbook Controversy," *The Diplomat*,

BIBLIOGRAPHY

April 4, 2015, https://web.archive.org/web/*/http://thediplomat.com/2015/04/south-koreas-history-textbook-controversy/.

Denzin, Norman K., and Yvonna S. Lincoln. "Introduction: The Discipline and Practice of Qualitative Research." In *The SAGE Handbook of Qualitative Research*, edited by Norman K. Denzin and Yvonna S. Lincoln, 3rd ed., 1–32. Thousand Oaks: Sage, 2005.

Derrida, Jacques. *The Gift of Death and Literature in Secret*. Second Edition. Chicago: University of Chicago Press, 1995.

Dey, Ian. "Grounded Theory." In *Qualitative Research Practice*, edited by Clive Seale, Giampietro Gobo, Jaber F. Gubrium, and David Silverman, 80–96. London: SAGE, 2007.

Doehring, Carrie. *The Practice of Pastoral Care: A Postmodern Approach*. Louisville, Ky.: Westminster John Knox Press, 2006.

Dykstra, Robert C. *Images of Pastoral Care: Classic Readings*. St. Louis, Mo.: Chalice, 2005.

Edwards, Paul, General editor, ed. *Body, Mind, and Death, Readings Selected, Edited, and Furnished with an Introductory Essay by Antony Flew*. Problems of Philosophy Series. New York: Macmillan, 1964.

Erikson, Erik H. *Identity, Youth, and Crisis*. New York: W.W. Norton, 1968.

Farrington, Debra K. *One like Jesus: Conversations on the Single Life*. Chicago: Loyola, 1999.

Fiorenza, Elisabeth Schüssler. *Discipleship of Equals: A Critical Feminist Ekklēsia-Logy of Liberation*. New York: Crossroad, 1993.

———. "Women in the Early Christian Movement." In *Womanspirit Rising: A Feminist Reader in Religion*, edited by Carol P Christ and Judith Plaskow. San Francisco: Harper & Row, 1979.

Flax, Jane. *Thinking Fragments: Psychoanalysis, Feminism, and Postmodernism in the Contemporary West*. Berkeley: University of California Press, 1990.

Foucault, Michel. *Discipline and Punish: The Birth of the Prison*. Translated by Alan Sheridan. 2nd Vintage Books ed. New York: Vintage, 1995.

———. "From What Is Enlightenment." In *Postmodernism: A Reader*, edited by Patricia Waugh, 96–108. London: Edward Arnold, 1992.

———. *Power/Knowledge: Selected Interviews and Other Writings, 1972–1977*. 1st American ed. New York: Pantheon, 1980.

Freedman, Jill, and Gene Combs. *Narrative Therapy: The Social Construction of Preferred Realities*. New York: Norton, 1996.

Gadamer, Hans-Georg. "The Universality of the Hermeneutical Problem." In *Philosophical Hermeneutics*, edited and translated by David E. Linge, 3–17. Berkeley: University of California Press, 1976.

Gaillardetz, Richard R. "Foreword." In *Ecclesiology and Exclusion: Boundaries of Being and Belonging in Postmodern Times*, edited by Dennis M. Doyle, Timothy J. Furry, and Pascal D. Bazzell. Maryknoll, N.Y.: Orbis, 2012.

Geertz, Clifford. *Local Knowledge: Further Essays in Interpretive Anthropology*. New York: Basic, 1983.

Gergen, Kenneth J. *An Invitation to Social Construction*. Revised edition. Los Angeles; London: SAGE, 2009.

———. "The Postmodern Adventure." *The Family Therapy Networker* 16, no. 6 (December 1992): 52, 56–57.

———. *The Saturated Self: Dilemmas of Identity in Contemporary Life.* New York: Basic Books, 1991.

———. "The Social Constructionist Movement in Modern Psychology." *American Psychologist* 40, no. 3 (March 1985): 266–75.

Gibbs, Eddie., and Ryan K. Bolger. *Emerging Churches: Creating Christian Community in Postmodern Cultures.* Grand Rapids, MI.: Baker Academic, 2005.

Gilligan, Carol. *In a Different Voice: Psychological Theory and Women's Development.* Cambridge, MA.: Harvard University Press, 1982.

Graham, Elaine L. *Transforming Practice: Pastoral Theology in an Age of Uncertainty.* London: Mowbray, 1996.

Graham, Larry Kent. *Care of Persons, Care of Worlds: A Psychosystems Approach to Pastoral Care and Counseling.* Nashville: Abingdon Press, 1992.

———. "From Relational Humanness to Relational Justice: Reconceiving Pastoral Care and Counseling." In *Pastoral Care and Social Conflict*, edited by Pamela D. Couture and Rodney J. Hunter, 220–34. Nashville: Abingdon Press, 1995.

Greider, Kathleen J., Gloria A. Johnson, and Kristen J. Leslie. "Three Decades of Women Writing for Our Lives." In *Feminist and Womanist Pastoral Theology*, edited by Bonnie J. Miller-McLemore and Brita L. Gill-Austern, 21–50. Nashville: Abingdon Press, 1999.

Gutiérrez, Gustavo. *A Theology of Liberation: History, Politics, and Salvation.* Maryknoll, N.Y.: Orbis Books, 1973.

Hanson, Norwood Russell. *Patterns of Discovery; An Inquiry into the Conceptual Foundations of Science.* Cambridge, England: Univ. Press, 1958.

Hare-Mustin, Rachel T. "Discourses in the Mirrored Room: A Postmodern Analysis of Therapy," *Family Process* 33 (1994): 19–35.

Hauerwas, Stanley. *The Peaceable Kingdom: A Primer in Christian Ethics.* Notre Dame, Ind.: University of Notre Dame Press, 1983.

Hess, Carol Lakey. *Caretakers of Our Common House: Women's Development in Communities of Faith.* Nashville, TN: Abingdon Press, 1997.

Hoffman, Lynn. "A Constructivist Position for Family Therapy," *The Irish Journal of Psychology* 9 (1988): 110–29.

———. "Constructing Realities: An Art of Lenses." *Family Process* 29, no. 1 (March 1, 1990): 1–12.

Holifield, E. Brooks. *A History of Pastoral Care in America: From Salvation to Self-Realization.* Nashville: Abingdon Press, 1983.

Hsu, Albert Y. *Singles at the Crossroads: A Fresh Perspective on Christian Singleness.* Downers Grove, IL.: InterVarsity Press, 1997.

Isasi-Díaz, Ada María. *Mujerista Theology: A Theology for the Twenty-First Century.* Maryknoll, N.Y.: Orbis Books, 1996.

———. "Solidarity: Love of Neighbor in the 21st Century." In *Lift Every Voice: Constructing Christian Theologies from the Underside*, edited by Susan Brooks Thistlethwaite and Mary Potter. Engel, Revised and Expanded edition., 30–39, 305–7. San Francisco: Harper & Row, 1998.

Izuzquiza, Daniel. *Rooted in Jesus Christ: Toward a Radical Ecclesiology.* Grand Rapids, MI.: William B. Eerdmans Pub. Co., 2009.

Justes, Emma. "Women." In *Clinical Handbook of Pastoral Counseling*, edited by Robert J. Wicks, Richard D. Parsons, and Donald Capps. New York: Paulist Press, 1985.

BIBLIOGRAPHY

Kang, Namsoon. "Theology from a Space Where Postcolonialism and Feminism Intersect." In *Postcolonial Theology*, edited by Hille Haker, Luiz Carlos Susin, and Eloi Messi Metogo. Concilium 2013/2. London: SCM Press, 2013.

Kant, Immanuel. "An Answer to the Question: What Is Enlightenment?" In *Postmodernism: A Reader*, edited by Patricia Waugh, 89–95. London: Edward Arnold, 1992.

Kegan, Robert. *In over Our Heads: The Mental Demands of Modern Life*. Cambridge, MA.: Harvard University Press, 1994.

Kuhn, Thomas S. *The Structure of Scientific Revolutions*. 50th Anniversary edition. Chicago: The University of Chicago Press, 1962.

Kujawa-Holbrook, Sheryl A. "Love and Power: Antiracist Pastoral Care." In *Injustice and the Care of Souls: Taking Oppression Seriously in Pastoral Care*, edited by Sheryl A. Kujawa-Holbrook and Karen Brown Montagno, 13–27. Minneapolis: Fortress Press, 2009.

Kujawa-Holbrook, Sheryl A., and Karen Brown Montagno. "Introduction." In *Injustice and the Care of Souls: Taking Oppression Seriously in Pastoral Care*, edited by Sheryl A. Kujawa-Holbrook and Karen Brown Montagno, 1–2. Minneapolis: Fortress Press, 2009.

Kvale, Steinar, and Svend Brinkmann. *InterViews: Learning the Craft of Qualitative Research Interviewing*. Thousand Oaks, CA: Sage Publications, 2015.

Lakoff, George, and Mark Johnson. *Metaphors We Live by*. Chicago: University of Chicago Press, 1980.

Landgraf, John R. *Creative Singlehood and Pastoral Care*. Philadelphia: Fortress Press, 1982.

———. *Singling: A New Way to Live the Single Life*. Louisville: Westminster/John Knox Press, 1990.

Lartey, Emmanuel Y. *In Living Color: An Intercultural Approach to Pastoral Care and Counseling*. London; New York: Jessica Kingsley Publishers, 2003.

———. *Postcolonializing God: New Perspectives on Pastoral and Practical Theology*. London: SCM Press, 2013.

LeDoux, Joseph E. *The Emotional Brain: The Mysterious Underpinnings of Emotional Life*. New York: Simon & Schuster, 1996.

Lester, Andrew D. *Hope in Pastoral Care and Counseling*. Louisville: Westminster John Knox Press, 1995.

Lipsky, Suzanne. "Internalized Oppression," In *Resisting Racism: An Action Guide*, edited by Gerald L. Mallon, 94–99. San Francisco: The National Association of Black and White Men Together, 1991.

Lyotard, Jean-François. *The Postmodern Condition: A Report on Knowledge*. Translated by Geoff Bennington and Brian Massumi. Theory and History of Literature v.10. Minneapolis: University of Minnesota Press, 1984.

———. *The Postmodern Explained: Correspondence, 1982–1985*. Edited by Julian Pefanis and Morgan Thomas. Translated by Don Barry, Bernadette Maher, Julian Pefanis, Virginia Spate, and Morgan Thomas. Minneapolis: University of Minnesota Press, 1993.

MacIntyre, Alasdair. *After Virtue: A Study in Moral Theory*. Notre Dame, IN.: University of Notre Dame Press, 1981.

Madigan, Stephen. *Narrative Therapy*. Washington, D.C: American Psychological Association, 2011.

———. "The Politics of Identity: Considering Community Discourse in the Externalizing of Internalized Problem Conversations," *Journal of Systemic Therapies* 15, No.1, Spring (1996): 47–61.
Martel, Yann. *Life of Pi*. New York: Mariner Books, 2001.
McFague, Sallie. *Models of God: Theology for an Ecological, Nuclear Age*. Philadelphia: Fortress Press, 1987.
McLeod, John. *Narrative and Psychotherapy*. Thousand Oaks, CA: Sage Publications, 1997.
———. "Narrative Thinking and the Emergence of Postpsychological Therapies," *Narrative Inquiry* 16, No.1 (2006): 201–10.
Miller-McLemore, Bonnie J. *Christian Theology in Practice: Discovering a Discipline*. Grand Rapids, MI.: W.B. Eerdmans Publishing Company, 2012.
———. "Pastoral Theology as Public Theology: Revolutions in the 'Fourth Area.'" In *Pastoral Care and Counseling: Redefining the Paradigms*, edited by Nancy J. Ramsay, 45–64. Nashville: Abingdon Press, 2004.
———. "The Living Human Web: Pastoral Theology at the Turn of the Century." In *Through the Eyes of Women: Insights for Pastoral Care*, edited by Jeanne Stevenson Moessner, 9–26. Minneapolis: Fortress Press, 1996.
Miller-McLemore, Bonnie J. "The Living Human Web: Pastoral Theology at the Turn of the Century." In *Through the Eyes of Women: Insights for Pastoral Care*, edited by Jeanne Stevenson Moessner, 9–26. Minneapolis: Fortress Press, 1996.
Montagno, Karen Brown. "Midwives and Holy Subversives: Resisting Oppression in Attending the Birth of Wholeness." In *Injustice and the Care of Souls: Taking Oppression Seriously in Pastoral Care*, edited by Karen Brown Montagno and Sheryl A. Kujawa-Holbrook, 3–12. Minneapolis: Fortress Press, 2009.
Neuger, Christie Cozad. *CounselingWomen: A Narrative, Pastoral Approach*. Minneapolis: Fortress Press, 2001.
Niebuhr, H. Richard. *The Meaning of Revelation*. Louisville, KY.: Westminster John Knox Press, 2006.
Nouwen, Henri J. M. *Reaching out: The Three Movements of the Spiritual Life*. Garden City, NY.: Doubleday, 1975.
Osmer, Richard Robert. *Practical Theology: An Introduction*. Grand Rapids, MI.: William B. Eerdmans Pub. Co., 2008.
Palmer, Parker J. *The Company of Strangers: Christians and the Renewal of America's Public Life*. New York: Crossroad, 1981.
Parry, Alan, and Robert E. Doan. *Story Re-Visions: Narrative Therapy in the Postmodern World*. New York: The Guilford Press, 1994.
Pattison, Stephen. *Pastoral Care and Liberation Theology*. Cambridge: Cambridge University Press, 1994.
Pattison, Stephen, and James Woodward. "An Introduction to Pastoral and Practical Theology." In *The Blackwell Reader in Pastoral and Practical Theology*, edited by James Woodward and Stephen. Pattison, 1–19. Oxford, UK ; Blackwell Publishers, 2000.
Patton, John. *Pastoral Care in Context: An Introduction to Pastoral Care*. Louisville, KY: Westminster/John Knox Press, 1993.
———. *Pastoral Care in Context: An Introduction to Pastoral Care*. Louisville: Westminster/John Knox Press, 1993.
Payne, Dorothy. *Singleness*. Philadelphia: Westminster Press, 1983.

Perkins, Pheme. "The Gospel of Mark: Introduction, Commentary, and Reflections." In *The New Interpreter's Bible: A Commentary in Twelve Volumes*, 507–733. Nashville: Abingdon Press, 1995.
Ramsay, Nancy J. "A Time of Ferment and Redefinition." In *Pastoral Care and Counseling: Redefining the Paradigms*, edited by Nancy J. Ramsay, 1–43. Nashville: Abingdon Press, 2004.
———. *Pastoral Diagnosis: A Resource for Ministries of Care and Counseling*. Minneapolis: Fortress Press, 1998.
Rapley, Tim. "Interviews." In *Qualitative Research Practice*, edited by Clive Seale, Giampietro Gobo, Jaber F. Gubrium, and David Silverman, 15–33. London: SAGE, 2007.
Riley, Gregory J. *The River of God: A New History of Christian Origins*. San Francisco: HarperCollins, 2001.
Riley, Lawrence E. "Factors Associated with Singlehood," *Journal of Marriage and the Family* 36, No. 3 (August 1974): 533–54.
Ruether, Rosemary Radford. *Sexism and God-Talk: Toward a Feminist Theology*. Boston: Beacon Press, 1983.
Saiving, Valerie. "The Human Situation: A Feminine View." In *Womanspirit Rising: A Feminist Reader in Religion*, edited by Carol P. Christ and Judith. Plaskow. San Francisco: Harper & Row, 1979.
Scheib, Karen D. *Challenging Invisibility: Practices of Care with Older Women*. St. Louis, MO.: Chalice Press, 2004.
Schwartzberg, Natalie, Kathy Berliner, and Demaris Jacob. *Single in a Married World: A Life Cycle Framework for Working with the Unmarried Adult*. New York: W.W. Norton & Co., 1995.
Smith, James K. A. *Who's Afraid of Postmodernism?: Taking Derrida, Lyotard, and Foucault to Church*. Grand Rapids, MI: Baker Academic, 2006.
Strunk, Orlo Jr. "A Prolegomenon to Counseling." In *Clinical Handbook of Pastoral Counseling*, edited by Robert J. Wicks, Richard D. Parsons, and Donald Capps, Expanded Edition., 1:14–25. New York: Paulist Press, 1985.
Swinton, John, and Harriet Mowat. *Practical Theology and Qualitative Research*. London: SCM, 2006.
West, Traci C. *Disruptive Christian Ethics: When Racism and Women's Lives Matter*. Louisville, KY.: Westminster John Knox Press, 2006.
White, Michael. *Narrative Practice: Continuing the Conversations*. New York: Norton, 2011.
———. "Pseudo-Encopresis: From Avalanche to Victory, from Vicious to Virtuous Cycles." In *Selected Papers*, 115–24. Adelaid, Australia: Dulwich Centre Publications, 1989.
———. "The Process of Questioning: A Therapy of Literary Merit?" In *Selected Papers*, 37–46. Adelaid, Australia: Dulwich Centre Publications, 1989.
White, Michael, and David Epston. *Narrative Means to Therapeutic Ends*. New York: Norton, 1990.
Wimberly, Edward P. *Recalling Our Own Stories: Spiritual Renewal for Religious Caregivers*. San Francisco: Jossey-Bass Publishers, 1997.

www.ingramcontent.com/pod-product-compliance
Lightning Source LLC
Chambersburg PA
CBHW071505150426
43191CB00009B/1424